Achieving

MEDICAL

Relaxation

Achieving Relaxation

GEDDES & GROSSET

This edition published by Geddes & Grosset, an imprint of
Children's Leisure Products Limited

© 1997 Children's Leisure Products Limited,
David Dale House, New Lanark ML11 9DJ, Scotland

First published 1997
Reprinted 1998,1999

Cover image by Marc Romanelli, courtesy of the Image Bank

ISBN 1 85534 347 9

Printed and bound in the UK

Contents

Achieving Relaxation

Stress

It is tempting to think that mental and physical stress is an ailment only of modern civilization; that our fast-paced urban lifestyles, straining under the relentless pressure of greater competitiveness and automation, has created a culture that lives on its nerves and feeds off crisis. This is a misconception; stress has been part of the human condition since the beginning of time. Like the air we breath, stress is an integral factor in human survival. Think about any challenge or stimuli, and stress has been a factor in our response. It is an active force that helps us rise to meet whatever everyday life throws at us and we thrive on taking up challenges, meeting that deadline and adapting to difficult situations.

Our response to stress is fast and effective, with our bodies going into what can best be described as 'fight or flight' mode. This means that when we initially register a challenge, our system undergoes a chain reaction of responses, which flood the body with enough strength and energy to either fight or take flight. This reaction has been a factor in human motivation since the earliest stages of our evolutionary history. Primitive human beings frequently faced life and death situations, when alertness, strength, speed and performance were vital and the primary, instinctive response was to survive. The type of challenges we all meet with today, however, are rather different and, as they rarely require a physical response, the body's reaction to the situation is often inappropriate.

The stresses of modern life are more complex and last over longer periods of time. In the past, challenges were instantaneous and had to be resolved instinctively; today, we are subjected to long-term emotional, occupational and environmental anxieties, which demand that we maintain a certain level of mental and physical health. We also have to prepare ourselves for times of crisis and events that test us to our fullest, such as divorce, redundancy, bereavement or illness. This means that we have to be poised to 'fight or flight' at another level and in a completely different way from our forebears.

The rapid way in which our society now changes and constantly throws up fresh challenges places an unhealthy strain on a system that may be struggling to keep up. The extra mental exertion we all expend just to keep 'on top of things' can create a bottleneck of energy as pressure builds up with nowhere to go. If nothing is done to relieve the situation the mechanisms we have for dealing with stress will eventually fail us, causing illness and exhaustion. It is vital, therefore, that we make a priority of finding ways of easing our bodies and minds out of 'fight or flight' mode and put ourselves on a better footing to be able to deal with the ever-changing pressures of the modern world.

In order to do this we need a greater understanding and awareness of how our bodies work. Our automatic physical response to danger or stress involves an intricate chain reaction of bodily and biochemical effects, involving the brain, the nervous system and hormones. As soon as we perceive a threat, our body explodes with energy and strength, and thousands of messenger hormones flood into the bloodstream to call the alarm. Our minds and bodies instantly become clear, alert and poised—ready for action. In this alarm reaction the main players are the lungs, brain, nervous system, muscle systems and hormones. Arousal is initially registered by the hypothalamus—a tiny crowd of cells at the base of the brain—which controls all automatic bodily functions and reactions. It releases chemicals, called endorphins, that act as natural painkillers. They dull the perception of pain and mental turmoil and help us to deal with the situation by blocking out factors that may otherwise prevent us from giving less than our peak performance.

Another chemical, called adrenaline, also helps us rise to the situation. It causes a quickening of the heart rate, a raising of blood pressure and a release of vital nutrients. It also creates muscle tension and affects breathing patterns, making them faster and shallower. But it is only one of the arousal hormones released by the adrenal gland near the kidneys. Noradrenaline, associated with positive ecstatic arousal, is also released into the bloodstream. The hormone cortisol is the agent involved in converting glycogen, stored in the liver, into blood sugar, creating instant energy and alerting the brain. The required surge of strength and effort comes from the male hormone testosterone. The thyroid gland also plays a part in our body's arousal response. It releases thyroxin, a hormone that stimulates the metabolic system, increasing its work rate and regulating oxygen consumption. This is vital, as the body anticipates that it will need increased resources of energy. Our digestive system also slows down during this process, as blood is diverted from the skin and stomach. We instinctively shut down the unnecessary systems in order to concentrate on mobilizing those vital for survival. As the digestive system is not deemed essential in a life or death situation it slows down and is effectively put on hold.

The body has undoubtedly evolved an efficient and prompt survival response but, as already mentioned, the goal posts have moved slightly. The causes of stress today are more complex and require more sophisticated solutions over a longer period of time. Our hormonal system suffers if it stays in 'fight' mode, as lengthy periods with our bodies on red-alert are not healthy for our mental or physical wellbeing, and what begins as a positive range of responses can eventually have a negative effect on health.

Research shows that we put our bodies on challenge alert without realizing it. Emotions such as anger, anxiety and impatience produce the same chemical reactions in the body as standing in front of a speeding car—our nervous systems and hormones will still be poised for 'fight or flight'. But the same physiology that leaves us feeling poised and alert can create havoc over a long period of time. A build-up of energy can lead us to become stress addicts, who become hooked on the adrenaline rush that stressful situations create. Or we can become so used to living on such a psychological and physical 'tilt' that we don't realize the harm it is causing.

Overdoses of adrenaline can cause irritability and agitation, while too much noradrenaline can leave us feeling disconnected and high. If arousal continues, the adrenal glands create anti-inflammatory chemicals to speed tissue repair, but cortisol will also suppress the immune system, leaving it vulnerable to illness and disease. Extra sodium is retained, endangering the performance of the cardiovascular system by causing fluid retention, raising the heart rate, increasing blood pressure and possibly inducing blood clots. Stomach ulcers are a classic symptom of stress, as the stomach cannot deal with the extra secretion of acid that occurs during times of turbulence. Acute and cumulative stress over a period of time can even cause death.

Less drastic but very common symptoms of stress include:

- increased pupil dilation
- perspiration
- increased heart rate and blood pressure (to get more blood to the muscles, brain and heart)
- rapid breathing (to take in more oxygen)
- muscle tenseness (in preparation for action)
- increased blood flow to the brain, heart and muscles (the organs that are most important in dealing with danger)
- less blood flow to the skin, digestive tract, kidneys and liver (where it is least needed in times of crisis)
- increased mental alertness and sensitivity (to assess the situation and act quickly)
- increased blood sugar, fats and cholesterol (for extra energy)
- a rise in platelets and blood-clotting factors (to prevent haemorrhage in case of injury)

This only accounts for the physical dangers of prolonged stress. The effects on emotional and physical wellbeing can be devastating, causing depression, anxiety, disorientation, panic, anger, insecurity and frustra-

The stress response

Physical reaction

Brain sends biochemical message that triggers adrenal gland

Pupils dilate

Mouth goes dry

Neck and shoulder muscles tense—large skeletal muscles contract, ready for action

Breathing becomes faster and shallower, supplying more oxygen to muscles

Heart pumps faster and blood pressure rises

Liver releases stored sugar to provide fuel for quick energy

Adrenaline and noradrenaline released

Digestion slows down or stops as blood is diverted away from the stomach

The body cools itself by perspiring: blood vessels and capillaries move close to skin surface

Muscles at opening of anus and bladder are relaxed

Symptom

Headaches, dizziness

Blurred vision

Difficulty swallowing

Aching neck, backache

Over-breathing, chest pains, tingling, palpitations, asthma

High blood pressure

Excess sugar in blood, indigestion

Nausea, indigestion, ulcers

Excess sweating, blushing

Frequent urination, diarrhoea

tion. Family breakdown, mental illness, alcoholism and drug dependency can all be caused by an accumulation of stress. No one is immune from stress, and we should all be aware of the danger signs and know how to deal with them. It is vital, therefore, that we learn more about ourselves and how our minds and bodies work, as only then will we be able to improve the way we handle stress and be able to lead healthier and more fulfilling lifestyles.

Relaxation Response

Just as the body has an automatic process to prepare it for a 'fight or flight' situation, it can also go into what is called the 'relaxation response'. This stage of low arousal is less well known than the body's red-alert status, and it initially takes a concentrated effort in order to experience it. The symptoms of the 'fight or flight' response—increased metabolic rate, quickened heart rate and faster breathing—are the direct opposite of those experienced by the body while in a state of deep relaxation.

We need to be truly relaxed for the process to begin and for the body to feel the full benefits. Two branches of the autonomic nervous system are responsible for most of the changes that take place. What is known as the 'sympathetic branch' slows down, allowing the 'parasympathetic branch' to assume a greater role, calming the body and mind and decreasing metabolism until it reaches a hypometabolic state—it was in a hypermetabolic state during the 'fight or flight' process.

During relaxation our bodies require very low maintenance, and the decrease in metabolism is similar only to that found in deep sleep. Our breathing becomes more regular and the heart rate decreases. In a sustained period of relaxation oxygen consumption actually falls below that measured during deep sleep. There is also a significant fall in blood lactate, a substance that enters the blood through the metabolism of skeletal muscles. This occurs three times faster during meditation than while sitting at rest. Blood pressure is also lowered, but only to normal pre-stress levels. All these things allow the body to recover from the strains placed on it by everyday life.

The relaxation response also elicits a marked alteration in brain activity. The brain emits four types of waves, each with its own rhythm. Beta waves signify everyday conscious rhythms; delta waves are present during sleep; theta waves appear while in a dreamlike state; and alpha waves are more prominent when the mind is active, yet relaxed. Effective meditation manufactures a predominance of alpha and theta waves—signifying a state of restfulness and deep relaxation, where the mind is alert but not strained or confused. These waves appear almost as soon as the body starts to relax, increasing in frequency as the process intensifies, allowing clearer and more constructive thinking.

A prolonged period of relaxation will also increase the body's secretion of particular mood-altering chemicals, known as neurotransmitters. One of these, serotonin, is a powerful hormone that is associated with feelings of happiness and contentment. Recent medical research suggests that a deficiency in this hormone is a contributory factor in cases of clinical depression.

Environmental Stress

We all have different reactions to stress, and experience helps us to develop our own methods of dealing with it. While some of us may lead *less* stressful lives, it is impossible to lead a completely stress-free life, as things happen to all of us unexpectedly and 'out of the blue'. The trick comes in weeding out as much of the trivial stress as possible and learning how to control our response to unavoidable, accumulative stress. If we can do this then we can be better prepared for the surprises life springs on us and learn to enjoy rising to the challenges they present.

All of us will have times in our lives that cause us great distress and leave us feeling unable to go on. Bereavement, family break-up and redundancy are devas-

Life Events and the Pace of Change

In the following table of stressful events, compiled by two American doctors, T. H. Holmes and R. H. Rahe (*Journal of Psychosomatic Research*, No. 11, 1967), specific events are weighted on a scale from 0 to 100. Scores of about 300 supposedly indicate a major life crisis, scores of 200 to 299 a moderate life crisis, and 100 to 199 a mild life crisis.

Event	Life change units
Death of a spouse	100
Divorce	73
Marital separation	65
Imprisonment	63
Death of a close relation	63
Personal injury or illness	53
Marriage/engagement/cohabitation	50
Loss of job	47
Marital reconciliation	45
Retirement	45
Illness in the family	44
Pregnancy	44
Sexual problems	39
Birth of a child	39
Business readjustment	39
Change in financial state	38
Death of a close friend	37
Change to a different type of work	36
Large mortgage or loan	31
Foreclosure of mortgage or loan	31
Change in job responsibilities	29
Son or daughter leaving home	29
Outstanding personal achievement	28
Beginning or end of school or college	26
Change in living conditions	25
Moving house	20
Change of school or college	20
Holiday	13
Christmas	12

tating events, but even moving house or changing jobs, usually seen as positive occasions, can produce high levels of stress. This is because stress doesn't just occur when we feel angry or are in grief. Welcomed events can be just as stressful if they create self-doubt or anxiety. Any sort of change, with relationships, homes or occupations, can induce stress, as human beings are essentially creatures of habit. The fight for homoeostasis— internal physiological equilibrium—is a relentless process and is made more difficult when drastic changes in the way we organize and live our lives are forced on us. The amount of stress we experience, therefore, is largely dependent on how we adapt to circumstances (*see* table on page 17).

One of the most prevalent causes of stress is our immediate environment. Urban living, in particular, with its associated problems of inadequate housing, noise, pollution, crowding, violence and poverty creates some of the most cumulative and pervasive forms of stress. These factors affect how we live, work and play, and much may depend on the infrastructure of the location, transport provision, and our ability to spend time away from our environment. If we feel unable to escape our surroundings, even for a brief time, then feelings of helplessness can grow to the point where they become very damaging to our self-image and the way we interact with other people.

There are ways of improving how we live and deal with stress that most of us recognize only subconsciously. For example, our home to most of us is more than a place to eat and sleep. In an increasingly hostile society we use our home as an oasis of calm. In our own homes we can shut the door on the outside world and surround ourselves with our personal possessions, family and friends. The 'feathering the nest' syndrome is well documented—it is an instinctive need to create a comfortable environment, one where we can relax and be ourselves.

In creating comfort, space is one of the most important factors. We all have invisible boundaries that outline our personal space. But these are difficult to maintain when our personal space is constantly being invaded. We should all be able to retreat inside ourselves and find peace, but many of us experience a physical lack of space that has an affect on our mental wellbeing as overcrowding and lack of privacy make personal calm all the more difficult to achieve. Also, advances in technology have led to increasing numbers of people working from home, and in many instances this has put a further strain on space allocation, as work space is carved out of resources already stretched between family members and various activities.

Our individual space requirements depend heavily on what we are used to. In Hong Kong, for example, where overcrowding is the norm, what most of us are used to in Britain would look positively luxurious. Building and space cost money, however, and in all societies those with lower incomes are usually restricted in their choice of accommodation or, increasingly, deprived of it altogether. Without privacy and space, quality of life undoubtedly suffers, as certain activities such as meditation, relaxation or making love need uninterrupted peace and quiet.

Light is another important factor in determining the quality of our everyday lives. In the depths of winter most of us look forward to the long summer days ahead. This is because natural light is almost as vital for healthy living as the air we breath. It regulates levels of the hormone melanonin, which influences sleep, mood and the reproductive cycle. Our instinctive love of light and the sun explains our annual migration to hotter climates. A lack of daylight can influence the natural production of melanonin, creating lethargy and depression. SAD—seasonal affective disorder—is increasingly seen in the winter months. Sufferers feel antisocial, tired and depressed. To counter such feelings it is advisable to work beside windows and let as much daylight into the workplace or home as possible. Fluorescent lighting, the most unnatural from of light, should be avoided wherever possible. As artificial light is a necessary evil, it is best to use full spectrum lights, as they simulate daylight.

Colour can have a huge effect on our moods and ability to relax. Effective and intelligent use of colour is one of the easiest and cheapest ways to improve our surroundings. This is increasingly being recognized by health and education authorities, and more thought now goes into selecting the decor for classrooms, hospital wards and waiting rooms. Scientific research has also shown that colours can have physical as well as psychological effects. It has been found, for example, that exposure to red light can often raise blood pressure, while exposure to blue light can actually lower it.

Occupational Stress

The modern world thrives on the work ethic, and we are taught at a very early age to equate personal adequacy with material success and professional status. Few of us are immune to the pressures placed on us by society to desire things—bigger televisions, faster cars, exotic holidays—that are symbols of status. Advertising and marketing strategies tap into this competitive urge and create in us a need to go one better than people around us, in other words succumb to the 'keeping up with the Joneses' syndrome. This starts at an early age—basically in tandem with the learning process. The fear of failure and the challenge of peer pressure motivates us to work to achieve. In moderation, this can be healthy, as achievement goes hand in hand with self-esteem, but it also creates a cumulative stress that follows us from school to secondary education, through to our working lives.

For many of us, however, it is a struggle to keep up, and we often work unnecessarily long hours in difficult working conditions just to keep our heads above water. It has become a truism nowadays to say that no job is for life. Temporary employment contracts and the threat of unemployment are now features of more and more peoples' working lives, and many feel lucky to have a job at all. Society, therefore, is forcing us to change our expectations of how we work, and this is taking its toll on our physical and emotional security.

In coping with the structural changes of our working lives, it is vital to try to embrace the positives among the negatives. Flexitime, job sharing and increased communication through technology and the 'information superhighway', offer new ways of working, which, if we are able to adapt to them, can offer us greater freedoms. More emphasis on leisure time and recreation should also mean more time to relax and relate to family and friends. We are starting to see worth in activities not necessarily related to the working environment. This control can be used to create a healthy, more relaxed style of living. Stress is a plague of current working practices, and even if we can't change our overall working situation, there are certain steps we can take to de-stress our days.

There is a lot of truth in the saying that a messy desk portrays a messy mind. Being chronically disorganized can be debilitating at work, where lack of planning is one of the most common causes of stress. Stressful environments are minimized when we impose a form of structure that can offer security against problems appearing 'out of the blue'. Too inflexible a pattern would be impractical, but keeping a diary, writing lists and prioritizing duties all help to stem stressful situations. Writing down objectives, duties and activities helps to make them seem more tangible and surmountable. Don't try to overload your mind with too much information—if you are already stressed there is more chance of you forgetting vital references and data—but if you take steps to keep control of things then you will work more efficiently.

People have different tolerances for routine and variety. Some personalities thrive under the security of a routine working day. In many ways it can be quite liberating, as adhering to a pattern means that you can fully concentrate on one task at a time and not get in a muddle attempting things that there may not be adequate time for. On the other hand, too much routine can be boring and demoralizing and eat away at your enthusiasm for the job. Variety at work holds interest and enthusiasm, but too little structure leads to overloading, confusion and stress.

Most of us need to strike a balance between routine and variety in order to enjoy work and maintain levels of efficiency. Monotony can be broken by looking ahead and planning when to switch from one job to another. Perhaps there is a way to inject some variety into your tasks—can you open up your job description? Those suffering under too great a workload should learn to say 'no', and not be afraid of the consequences. Pacing yourself is one of the most vital practices in achieving a relaxed lifestyle. Learn when to stop and stand back from your activity, the odd moment of calm will increase efficiency when you do return to your task.

Most people suffer from time deprivation, as it is perhaps one of life's most precious commodities. We have to juggle everything—work, family, friends, leisure, eating and sleeping—in only twenty-four hours. Every day most of us have to strip demands on our time down to the essentials, and usually it is the time spent working and commuting that dictates how much we can give to other activities.

Time deprivation leaves us feeling harassed, hurried and guilty. It may also damage relationships, as it can mean breaking arrangements because we 'just don't have the time'. Some people make the situation worse— as the saying goes, 'less haste, more speed'. They will procrastinate and waste time worrying about commitments in their social life and deadlines at work. Often they take on too much and end up fulfilling few or none of their aims. Work will pile up and relationships suffer as commitments are neglected, and the individual is left feeling panicked and chaotic.

It can be very difficult to change habits formed over a lifetime. Often the best way is to recognize weak points in time management and learn to deal with them. Prioritize and look at the steps mentioned earlier for dealing with organization. Also, don't punish yourself for not having the time to do everything or be everywhere—it is not humanly possible or desirable.

Nutrition

Relaxation is virtually impossible if your body isn't maintained properly.

Food is the fuel we put into our bodies in order to survive, and exercise creates the process that turns it into energy. In times past, the equation was relatively easy to achieve—the balance between energy input and output occurred naturally. We burnt up a lot of energy just keeping warm and doing a lot of physical work. Today's society, with its increased automation and sedentary jobs, makes it more difficult to maintain any equilibrium. Western society offers us abundant food and warmth with minimum physical outlay, so it has become all the more important consciously to monitor the balance of our diets.

Being overweight or underweight can create serious health problems. Obesity can cause diabetes, high blood pressure and heart problems. Being underweight is no more desirable in terms of health. An underweight body can lack the energy and strength to carry out effectively its functions, leaving the individual tired and listless. Add bad habits such as smoking or excessive alcohol consumption to either of these conditions and it often becomes very difficult for the body to cope.

Food management is important not just when it comes to checking weight, it can also improve your ability to relax and cope with stress. Food affects every organ of our bodies, including the heart, lungs and brain. The correct diet will encourage fitness and energy, nourish nerves, feed muscles, improve circulation and breathing, and support the immune system. It will promote a general feeling of positiveness and calm.

The eating process itself can create a feeling of well-being. What, and how, we eat says a lot about our emotional state—think of how a baby is calmed by the act of feeding, even if it is not hungry. We instinctively link eating to nurturing, comfort and security. At one extreme, anorexia nervosa and bulimia nervosa are examples of how emotional distress can affect our relationship with food. Yet all of us skip meals or overeat when we are feeling under pressure. As the digestive system shuts down during periods of stress, this is particularly dangerous and can lead to stomach problems and 'executive' ulcers.

To guard against ill-health it is vital to be aware of your body's needs. Often this means re-educating your body in terms of nutrition and taste—it can take a while for a 'junked-out' palate to become accustomed to unprocessed foods. But information has never been more accessible. Nutritional education is now seen as a step in preventive medicine, and the general principles are easy to follow.

Every food has its own nutritional make-up and has a unique effect on the mechanics of your body. What each food does for you depends on its core attributes and composition, and it can either enhance or aggravate your sense of wellbeing.

There are some foods that, quite simply, are not good for you. It is important to cut back or drop these foods from your diet. Most people know that fat intake should be carefully monitored. Fats generally fall into two groups: saturated and unsaturated. Saturated fats are found in dairy produce, vegetable fats, palm oil, hard margarines, sauces and biscuits, and are the most dangerous. Polyunsaturated fats are a subgroup of unsaturated fats and are present in sunflower, corn and soya oil, nuts and soft margarines. Eating too much fat can lead to obesity, heart disease, strokes and heart attack. Polyunsaturated fats do not raise cholesterol levels in the same way as saturated fats, and they can also help to restore everyday wear and tear.

Most of us eat much more salt than is healthy. Part of the reason our intake is so high is that salt is present in most foods as a preservative, making it difficult to avoid. The dangers of high salt intake are similar to our responses to stress. It can induce high blood pressure, irritate the menstrual cycle and have a stimulating and weakening effect on the adrenal glands, muscles and nervous system.

Preservatives, antioxidants, colourings, raising agents, flavour enhancers and sweeteners, emulsifiers and stabilizers are all included in the 3500 different additives frequently used by food manufacturers. Some are natural and some are completely synthetic, and most are silently injected into our diet. It is difficult to check the label on everything we buy in the supermarket, but it is well worth the effort to make ourselves aware of what we are taking home. Some of these additives have been found to have negative effects on our health and emotional wellbeing, and the only way to guard against them is through conscious awareness and nutritional education.

Sugar is one of the most common food additives, and, unfortunately, it is also one of the most 'empty' of all foodstuffs. It induces a short-term boost of energy, but when we eat too much of it our adrenal glands are overloaded and become sluggish. This reduces our ability to relax and causes irritability and a lack of concentration. An overly high sugar intake will also strain our insulin-producing glands, perhaps inducing diabetes, or hypoglycaemia (*see* page 42). More obvious problems include obesity and tooth decay. These are particularly difficult problems for children to deal with, and parents must be aware of the dangers of placating a disruptive child with a bar of chocolate or a bag of sweets.

In small doses caffeine can be a good thing. Its initial effects are increased alertness and activity in the muscles, nervous system and heart. Unfortunately, people often use caffeine to fuel an already overloaded system, thinking that it will improve their performance. Too much caffeine has the same effects on the system as prolonged stress—anxiety, over-stimulation, headache, migraine, emotional instability, palpitations—and should be avoided wherever possible.

The amount of alcohol we consume can also create health problems and contribute to stress levels. A limited intake can actually be very beneficial—red wine in particular contains things that are very good for us—but taken in excess, alcohol will destroy organs as well our emotional wellbeing. Dependency on alcohol is a disease in itself, which can create great distress not only for the alcoholic but for his or her family and friends as well.

If you seek a more relaxed lifestyle, you should start by caring for yourself from the inside, and feed your body with only 'good' fuel. The general maxims of a healthy diet are to increase our intake of fruit, vegetables, carbohydrates and low fat proteins, such as fresh fish or lean meat. Fibre became a buzz word of the 1980s and it is still valued—but fortunately a healthy diet should preclude the need for endless bowls of bran.

Fat is essential but, as discussed, only in restricted quantities.

Of course, there are many foods that aid the mental and physical balance of our bodies. When we are under a lot of pressure and feel worn down by life, the body will benefit from supplements of substances that are devoured by a system under stress. Unfortunately, vitamins and nutrients can have a short shelf-life. Food has to be very fresh, as some vitamins are easily eroded by heat, light and storage. Overcooking can destroy the nutritional value of many foods, and it is always best to eat food raw or lightly cooked when possible. Buying organic food is another way of ensuring that our bodies get the nutrients they need.

Although nutrients are best taken in their most natural form, modern diets do not always allow this, and we often need to supplement our intake. It is now possible to obtain vitamins and minerals that are specifically targeted to help with stress. A deficiency of vitamin C is a common problem, as stress hampers our ability to create and absorb it. Such a deficiency can also damage our absorption of iron. Supplements of vitamin B6 are recommended when under stress, pregnant or during times of anxiety and worry. A lack of B6 can lead to physical and mental exhaustion. Zinc deficiency is a common sign of stress and can induce stomach problems, a breakdown of the immune system, poor healing, low appetite and fatigue. Iodine, linked to the thyroid gland, has a direct effect on the metabolic rate of the body, so a deficiency can cause exhaustion while supplements have a stimulant effect. For more information make time to visit your local health food shop or chemist—staff will be glad to advise.

It is important to keep your diet and dietary behaviour as balanced as possible. The demands of modern-day life sometimes make it difficult to adhere to a well-balanced diet. There will always be times when the processed, overcooked oven meal is just too convenient, or when you really don't have time to sit down for a bite. Given this inevitability, it is all the more important to monitor what you eat and to try to make up for the days when you do not have the time to prepare something more wholesome. This is the only way to let your body cope and to lessen any anxiety you may have about not eating properly.

Super Health Foods

There are certain foods that are super foods—packed full of nutritional value in such beautifully balanced forms that they are easy to assimilate. Much richer in specific nutrients than ordinary or processed food, if you incorporate these super foods into your diet, you will boost your energy levels and achieve a personal equilibrium that is one of the most basic—and long-lasting—aspects of relaxation in the truest sense of the word.

Almonds

Almonds are an important source of the minerals zinc, magnesium, potassium and iron, so that a small handful of the nuts can transform a light salad into a well-balanced meal. You should eat vitamin C-rich foods at the same time, because almonds also contain oxalic and phytic acid, which can prevent your absorption of this vitamin.

Apricots

The brighter the fruit, the more beta-carotene it contains, and apricots are very high in vitamin A. Dried apricots are a wonderful source of beta-carotene during the winter months.

Avocado Pears

Avocados are an almost complete food—so much so, that in some parts of the world babies are weaned using mashed avocado. They are rich in potassium and vitamin A.

Barley

This grain has a very high mineral content. It has lots of calcium, potassium and B-complex vitamins, making it especially useful for anyone suffering from stress or fatigue. Add a handful of barley to home-made chicken soup ('Jewish penicillin') for a soothing and nourishing meal. It also lowers the level of cholesterol in the body.

Beetroot

For hundreds of years, beetroot has been used as a folk remedy for anaemia and liver problems. It helps the digestive system—especially when grated raw, perhaps served with grated apple and carrot and dressed with lemon juice and olive oil. It is much better eaten in this way rather than drowned in vinegar.

Broccoli

Like other members of the crucifer family—cabbage, cauliflower, Brussels sprouts, etc—broccoli has a protective effect against disease. It is rich in vitamin C, iron, beta-carotene and folic acid. Like all green vegetables, it should be lightly cooked (steaming is ideal) to preserve most of its nutrients.

Carrots

A single carrot will supply all your vitamin A needs for a whole day. Nibbling carrot sticks is a much healthier pastime than grazing on salted peanuts and crisps. Research has shown that carrots have a protective effect against ultraviolet rays, so they can help you to look younger for longer as well.

Celery

According to Hippocrates, celery calms the nerves—
perhaps because of its high calcium content. It helps
eliminate waste via the urine, due to the effect it has on
the kidneys.

Cider Vinegar

Made by fermenting the juice of whole, fresh apples, cider vinegar's beneficial effects come from the high mineral content of apples. It is unusually high in potassium,
calcium, phosphorus, sodium and trace elements. It increases blood oxygenation, improves metabolism,
strengthens digestion and increases blood clotting ability. Two teaspoonfuls of cider vinegar in a glass of water
on an empty stomach first thing in the morning is helpful to people with weight problems.

Garlic

Like sprouts, garlic has been used as a cure-all for mil-
lennia. Inscriptions on the Great Pyramid at Gizeh in
Egypt mention garlic as one of the foods eaten by its
builders.

Some naturopaths believe that common infectious
diseases, like flu and bronchitis, are caused by an accumulation of toxins in the body that gradually under-
mines the functions of internal organs. Garlic has been
shown to be an excellent antiseptic. It was used with

amazing success in treating soldiers with infected wounds during both World Wars. In the Second World War, the wounds of British soldiers were treated with garlic. Some of the wounds were already gangrenous, but garlic checked the spread of the gangrene and resulted in the shedding of gangrenous tissue. As recently as 1965 the Russians flew 500 tons of garlic to Moscow to fight a flu epidemic, and some people still call garlic 'Russian penicillin'.

Garlic also helps clear fat accumulations from the blood vessels, lower cholesterol, and protect against bacterial and viral infections.

Grapes

Grapes are very cleansing and regenerating. Grape fasts—eating nothing but grapes and drinking water for a day or two—are a well-known method of detoxifying the body. They are an ideal food, not only for convalescents, but for anyone suffering from fatigue or depression,

Kelp

Kelp—or seaweed—is a wonderful source of iodine, which helps protect the body against the radioactivity in the atmosphere that contributes to early ageing. It is rich in B-complex vitamins, vitamins D, E and K, magnesium and calcium. It is particularly good for hair and nails.

Kelp tablets are not concentrated; they are simply dehydrated seaweed, so six or eight of them should be taken after each meal for good results.

Lecithin

Lecithin is important in maintaining a healthy nervous system and is vital in helping the body resist stress. Daily lecithin consumption means that body fats are converted into energy more quickly, and existing fat deposits will slowly disperse. It breaks up cholesterol so that it can pass through artery walls, and has been shown to increase immunity to virus infections and help prevent gallstones. It also helps to cleanse the liver and purify the kidneys and, because of its choline and unsaturated fatty acid content, it is very good indeed for the condition of the skin.

Lecithin can be bought in granule form from health food shops.

Mixed Three Seeds

Pumpkin, sunflower and sesame seeds, ground in a blender or coffee grinder in equal proportions, make a wonderful complete protein to sprinkle on salads or fruits. They are extremely rich in vitamins, and are excellent for hair and skin as well as general health. Pumpkin seeds are rich in B vitamins, phosphorus, iron and zinc. Sesame seeds are rich in magnesium and potassium and have been used for generations to treat fatigue, insomnia and sexual dysfunctions. They also contain more calcium than milk, cheese or nuts and are a good source of vitamin E. Sunflower seeds are rich in iron, the B-complex vitamins, magnesium and zinc.

Molasses

A tablespoonful of black-strap molasses supplies as much calcium as a glass of milk, as much iron as nine eggs, more potassium than any other food, and the B-complex vitamins in good balance. It is also rich in magnesium, vitamin E and copper, and is a very valuable food for women who tend to be anaemic. It is an alkali-forming food, beneficial for maintaining a proper acid-alkaline balance in the body. A tablespoon of molasses and the juice of half a lemon in a mug of hot water is a good way to start the day. It is also very good for the condition of your skin and hair.

Warning: Diabetics must not use molasses.

Oats

Oats are a uniquely soothing food for the nerves. They are amazingly high in calcium, potassium and magnesium, together with lots of B-complex vitamins, which are all vital to a healthy nervous system. They also help lower cholesterol levels. A bowl of porridge, perhaps with a spoonful of honey or molasses, makes a uniquely calming breakfast for a child on the morning of an exam.

Potatoes

Potatoes have a well-known soporific effect: they contain a substance very like chloroform. Research suggests that certain foods cause contentment and lifting of depression by altering brain chemistry in a similar way to drug therapy. To prevent downward mood swings, a chemical called serotonin must be present in the brain in proper amounts. The body makes serotonin from the amino acid tryptophan. Under ordinary circumstances, tryptophan has to compete with other amino acids to get into the brain. But when more carbohydrate than protein is eaten, tryptophan has much less trouble getting in. A potato is not only an ideal carbohydrate: a medium potato contains only about 90 fat-free calories, as well as vitamins A, C, B_1, B_6, niacin, iron, potassium and fibre. What could be more comforting or soothing than a creamy mass of freshly whipped up potato with a swirl of olive oil or a knob of fresh, cold butter melting on top?

Rabbit

Much lower in fat than beef or lamb, rabbit—especially wild rabbit, if you can get it—makes delicious slow-cooked dishes to warm and soothe on a cold winter's evening. Rabbit with prunes and Guinness is bursting with nutrients. Serve with barley instead of rice or potatoes for the ultimate nourishing and relaxing treat.

Sprouted Grains

Sprouted grains and seeds have been used in diets for thousands of years, especially by the Chinese. They are amazing powerhouses of live food nourishment. They are rich in vitamins A, C, D, E, K and B complex, in calcium, phosphorus, potassium, magnesium, iron, high quality protein and enzymes. Sprouts are rich in vitality factors because, unlike most vegetables, they are eaten at the peak of their freshness—when they are still growing.

Sprouts contain an amazing quantity of enzymes. As we age, our bodies become less efficient at producing enzymes from food, which often leads to indigestion or flatulence. Sprouts, by giving us lots of enzymes, produce more efficient digestion and improved metabolism of food into energy. As well as being highly nutritious, sprouts are extremely low in calories.

How to grow sprouts:

Seeds to sprout include alfalfa (considered to be the richest in minerals), wheat, mung beans, buckwheat, lentils, sesame seeds, soya beans and chickpeas.

Put a heaped tablespoonful of seeds or grains into a

jar, cover it with lukewarm water and leave it overnight. In the morning, covering the jar with a piece of muslin or cheesecloth held in place with a rubber band, pour off the water and rinse the seeds in fresh lukewarm water (not hot—or you will kill them). Pour off the excess water through the cloth and put the jar on the windowsill. In the evening, rinse again and pour off excess. Repeat the rinsing twice a day, and, in three to six days—depending on the kind of seeds used—you will have sprouts to sprinkle on your salads or steam lightly and enjoy with a sprinkling of olive oil and lemon juice. Patent plastic sprouters are now available that make sprouting even easier.

Spirulina
Spirulina is a blue-green, single-celled alga, microscopic in size and spiral in shape—hence its name. It thrives in warm alkaline lakes such as Lake Texcoco in Mexico. It was so highly valued by the Aztecs that it was used as currency.

The B_{12}, folic acid and chlorophyll content of spirulina makes it useful in the treatment of anaemia and liver disorders.

Spirulina is helpful in weight control. Its protein contains a high proportion of the amino acid phenylalanine, which is transformed into brain neurotransmitter substances that control appetite, energy level and mood.

The appetite is curbed and a state of wellbeing is maintained. The usual dose is three tablets taken half an hour before each meal.

Wheat Germ

Wheat germ is the richest known source of vitamin E. It is also rich in magnesium, copper, manganese, calcium and phosphorus. Sprinkled on yoghurt or cereal, it a superb source of protein. But it is rich in fat—a tablespoonful a day is enough.

Hypoglycaemia

If you are suffering from hypoglycaemia—often called 'the great imitator' because it mimics so many mental and emotional disorders—you will find it almost impossible to relax completely. A large proportion of patients receiving psychotherapy—more than half, it is thought—are in fact hypo-glycaemic. Symptoms include: irritability, exhaustion, nervousness, depression, faintness and dizziness, cold sweats, headaches, confusion, heart palpitations, lack of sex drive, lack of concentration, blurred vision, phobias and allergies.

Hypoglycaemia, or low sugar levels in the blood, was discovered in 1924 by Dr Seale Harris. At that time it was called hyperinsulinism because it was thought to be caused by excessive insulin secretion due to an overactive pancreas. The excess insulin causes rapid up-take of glucose by the cells and tissues of the body, leav-ing the blood depleted of glucose. When glucose is in short supply, cell function is impaired, leading to physi-cal and mental problems.

Low blood sugar may impair mental health even more than physical health because it deprives the brain and nervous system of oxygen.

During digestion, all ingested carbohydrates (sugars and starches) are converted to glucose, which is the only carbohydrate the body can use. After a meal, particu-larly one with a high sugar content, surges of glucose enter the blood, causing the pancreas to secrete insulin. Insulin causes rapid uptake of glucose by almost all of the tissues of the body and also promotes the conversion of excess glucose to glycogen, a more compact form of glucose that can be stored in the liver for future use. The pancreas, however, is only part of the mechanism that controls blood sugar. The whole process originates in glucoreceptor (glucose-sensitive) nerve cells in the brain from which impulses travel to the pituitary gland, adrenal glands, liver and finally the pancreas. In this so-phisticated sugar-control chain, there are also hormones that convert glycogen back to glucose to raise the blood glucose level. The hormones that do this are glucagon, also secreted by the pancreas, and adrenaline, secreted by the adrenal glands. In this way, opposing forces are constantly at work, balancing each other, so that blood sugar levels are kept within fairly narrow limits. But they do not always succeed and, if the blood sugar level gets too low, hypoglycaemia occurs.

Some people inherit or develop an overactive pancreas, which secretes excessive amounts of insulin even when only small amounts of sugar enter the blood. Sometimes, the pancreas may react slowly and insulin does not enter the blood until the sugar level has already fallen—this is retarded hypoglycaemia. On the other hand, secretion of glucagon and adrenaline, the hormones that balance the action of insulin, may be too low. Hypoglycaemia can also be caused by allergies or an imbalance in the autonomic nervous system. Other causes are excessive consumption of alcohol, tobacco, coffee, overeating and emotional stress. Whatever the reason, hypoglycaemia develops when the delicate balance of the systems and substances that control blood sugar is upset.

Theoretically, sugar would appear to be the ideal food to raise blood sugar levels. But sugar is the one food that hypoglycaemics should avoid. In fact, sugar will eventually contribute to lower blood sugar levels.

When we eat sugar, it is readily absorbed into the blood, where it raises blood sugar levels, triggering the pancreas to secrete insulin, which will cause glucose to be absorbed into the tissues. Insulin, because it breaks down much more slowly than sugar, remains circulating in the blood for several hours, lowering blood sugar level even lower than the original level. It triggers the hypoglycaemic symptoms again, creating a craving for more sugar. So the hypoglycaemic eats more sugar, which deepens the vicious circle. The high consumption of refined sugar is thought to be the main cause for the higher rates of hypoglycaemia.

When we start consuming huge amounts of white sugar, our pancreas becomes highly stressed. The occasional binge can be dealt with, but when large intakes of refined carbohydrates are the norm, the strain on the sugar-regulating mechanism becomes intolerable and it breaks down. The pancreas may develop an over-sensitivity to sugar and produce more insulin than is really needed to keep a normal sugar level. This results in a consistently low blood sugar level, which deprives the brain and the nervous system of vital oxygen and produces all the symptoms of hypoglycaemia.

Coffee (especially when taken with sugar) and soft drinks that are high in caffeine contribute to hypoglycaemia by acting on the adrenal glands, brain and liver while sugar is flooding the blood stream. Too much salt in the diet depletes potassium and stress and allergies overtax the adrenal glands. Vitamin deficiencies—particularly zinc, chromium, B vitamins, magnesium, potassium and vitamin E—also contribute to hypoglycaemia. So it is easy to see that the condition, which has such a devastating effect on so many people's equilibrium, is mainly a nutritional disorder.

The influence of sugar in the body goes far beyond carbohydrate metabolism. Fatty acid synthesis and oxidation, cholesterol synthesis and the accumulation of ketone bodies, are all in part controlled by the rate at which glucose is broken down within cells.

Refined sugar causes more build-up of fat than any other carbohydrate except alcohol. This, in turn, means a greater susceptibility to heart attacks and high blood pressure.

Changes in Western eating habits over the last couple of generations have been in the direction of fewer complex carbohydrates (cereals, potatoes etc) and more simple sugars.

Life stresses are also an important factor. Under conditions of stress, more adrenaline is secreted, releasing more sugar from the liver. Repeated stress can impair the function of the adrenal glands, reducing the body's ability to cope with stress. When this happens we get depressed easily, and also develop hypoglycaemic symptoms. Persistent stress is a major cause of depression.

Like diabetes, hypoglycaemia is diagnosed by means of a glucose tolerance test, which can be arranged through your doctor.

A healthy diet, which means only rarely consuming simple sugars or junk food, can keep hypoglycaemia at bay. Plenty of complex carbohydrates and vegetables, together with a good multivitamin and multimineral supplement will go a long way towards this.

There are some simple rules that will improve your diet. These are not to be followed slavishly of course, the occasional sweet treat will do little harm if the main-stay of your diet is good, fresh food.

1 Eat good quality food

If we are what we eat, we do not want to put substandard materials into our bodies. Stick to good, natural foods that have nourished people for generations: fresh vegetables and fruit; fresh fish; poultry, game, beef and lamb—reared organically, if possible; wholegrains; nuts; seeds; pulses, free-range eggs; cold-pressed oils; cheeses, butter and milk.

2 Eat regularly

It is better to eat four or five small meals spread throughout the day, rather than starving all day and bingeing on a large dinner at night. This is also very important for keeping your blood sugar level constant.

3 Eat fresh foods in season

It is sensible to eat a really fresh, locally grown carrot,

rather than some green beans that have been flown from Kenya and will have lost some nutrients in transit. It is also cheaper. Local produce is also more likely to have been harvested at its peak. Exotic fruits and vegetables are often chemically treated to ripen them artificially in transit.

4 Avoid over-processed and refined foods

Use wholemeal rather than white flour and eat brown rice rather than white. Try not to eat mass-produced cakes and pastries and sugary cereals. It is easy to munch your way through a packet of high-fat, high-salt crisps merely out of habit, without enjoying them. If you change your diet for a healthier one, after a while the artificial cream gateau will lose its appeal.

5 Eat in moderation

Exercise a little self control. It is not necessary to weigh every wedge of cheese or count out the strands of spaghetti. Listen to your body. A glass of wine occasionally is fine—but not if you go on to down the entire bottle.

6 Eat slowly and calmly

Take time to sit down and enjoy your meal. Grabbing some food and bolting it, when short of time, will play havoc with your digestion.

7 Don't mix foods that fight

All foods belong in one of three groups: protein, starch and neutral. Many people believe that a particularly harmonious way of eating is one in which protein and starch foods are not eaten at the same meal. People who follow this regime (sometimes called the Hay system after Dr Hay who developed it) eat neutral foods with any of the protein foods or any of the starch foods. They aim to eat one starch meal, one protein meal and one made up mainly of fruit, vegetables and salads every day. Four hours should be allowed between starch and protein meals.

If you would like to try this eating plan, the chart opposite shows which foods can be combined.

It is a good idea to begin meals with a salad; this will encourage your digestion to work efficiently, as well as curbing your appetite. Base your meals as much as possible around fresh fruit and vegetables. At first it may seem strange giving up classic combinations like fish and chips or shepherd's pie. But it is possible to eat very enjoyably—from a delicious mushroom and barley casserole, to a corn-fed chicken, cooked with olive oil and tarragon, and served with a wide range of appetizing vegetables and a glass of good wine.

Following this regime, many people are pleasantly surprised to find that they lose weight without really trying.

The three food groups

Protein	Neutral	Starch
meat	all vegetables	potatoes
poultry	except potatoes,	yams
game	yams and	sweetcorn
fish	sweetcorn	bread
shellfish	all nuts except	flour
eggs	peanuts	oats
all fruit except those	butter	wheat
in the starch group	cream	barley
all dried fruit except	cream cheese	rice
raisins, which are	yoghurt and milk	millet
neutral	(these are protein	rye
tomatoes (but when	foods, but their	buckwheat
cooked their acidity	protein content is	very sweet fruits
is increased,	low and they can	such as ripe pears,
making them	be used in very	bananas, papaya,
unsuitable for	small amounts	mango and sweet
eating with starch	only with starch	grapes
foods)	foods)	beer
peanuts	cold-pressed	
soya beans	sesame	
tofu	sunflower and olive	
milk	oils	
yoghurt	all salad stuffs	
all cheeses except	lentils	
cream cheese	dried split peas	
wine	dried or tinned	
cider	beans, chickpeas	
	etc	
	seeds and sprouted	
	seeds	
	herbs and spices	
	raisins	
	honey	
	maple syrup	

Exercise

Getting the diet right is only part of the picture. It is impossible to overestimate the significance of exercise in a healthy and relaxed lifestyle. If a body is never pushed beyond its regular pace, relaxation periods will invariably have less benefit. Exercise doesn't just promote an increase in physical fitness; people who exercise regularly can enjoy a range of secondary benefits.

Regular exercise improves sleep, reduces headaches, creates a feeling of wellbeing, and increases concentration and stamina. Endorphins are released into the brain during exercise and these chemicals promote a sense of positivity and happiness that will last for some time after the actual activity. This is an effective tool in the fight against depression and a vital move in the preparation for a relaxed life.

People are often accused of putting too much time into their careers or families, and strenuous physical activity is a great antidote to that. In today's society there is a general emphasis on sedentary lifestyles, and it is a trend that shows little sign of slowing down. This makes it difficult to find an appropriate outlet for mental negativity and accumulated physical frustration. Physical exertion is great for releasing the toxic emotions that threaten a relaxed sense of wellbeing. You can thrash out tension, anger, frustration and aggression, exercising your mental muscles along with your physical ones.

Exercise is a personal thing. Just as you will prefer one relaxation method over another, you probably won't like all forms of activity. Your preferences will be affected by your individual personality, physical capabilities and the time you have available. Realistically tailoring your activity to your lifestyle is the best way to ensure that the exercise is kept up.

Skilled sports such as skiing or golf are obviously more appealing if you have the time to invest in learning the game and developing your ability to a certain level. Highly competitive sports such as squash should be viewed with caution if you already have an exceptionally stressful lifestyle. Most experts would advise some form of noncompetitive exercise, like swimming, weight-training or walking, for those with limited time and resources. Even as little as twenty minutes a day put aside for such activities will be of great benefit.

It is important not to push yourself too hard in the beginning, especially if you are not used to regular exercise. It is always a good idea to seek advice on which form of sport to take up and to consult your doctor before you begin. Ease yourself into an exercise programme, as doing too much too soon could lead to physical exhaustion or injury. Also remember that the body benefits more from short periods of regular exercise than from infrequent bursts.

Aerobic Exercises

Aerobic activities include swimming, long-distance running, bicycling, rowing, cross-country skiing and even walking—if it is brisk enough. These differ from the other sorts of exercise because they demand your body's efficient use of oxygen throughout the whole time you are doing them.

Oxygen is the ignition factor in the burning of energy from the foods you eat. A good supply is always necessary for your body's metabolic processes to take place efficiently. When your cells—particularly your brain cells—have a good supply, you have stamina, feel well and don't tire easily. If you often feel tired, become depressed easily and have trouble concentrating, it is likely that your body is not getting enough exercise. Taking aerobic exercise will change all that. Any movement of sustained rhythm that puts a constant demand on your heart—raising your pulse rate to between 120 and 160 beats a minute—will bring about several important changes in your body:

It will tone your muscles and improve your circulation. It will increase the number and the size of the blood vessels that carry blood from your heart all over your body so you will have better transport of oxygen. It will increase your body's capacity to take in oxygen by strengthening the chest wall and making you breathe more easily. This oxygen will generate energy. It will make your bones, joints and ligaments stronger so they are more resistant to injury. It will increase the level of energy-rich compounds and enzymes in your body, making it easier for you to use the nutrients in your food. As the efficiency of your heart increases, pumping more blood with each beat, your basic pulse rate will decline.

Walking

Walking is often overlooked as an aerobic activity. A brisk, purposeful walk will improve your muscle condition, your circulation and your posture.

All you need is a good pair of strong shoes and a lightweight, waterproof jacket. Start off by walking for thirty minutes a day. Walk fast enough to make yourself a little out of breath and vary your route so you are not walking on flat ground all the time.

After a week or two, you can increase the time you walk to about forty-five minutes. By now you should be seeing the benefits: you will probably be sleeping better, your concentration will be sharper and you will feel better balanced emotionally.

Walking is an ideal aerobic exercise because you can do it wherever you are—in the country or the city. You need no equipment to measure your progress—you do not need to stop and take your pulse. Get into the habit of walking briskly every day and you will be rewarded with a fit body, glowing skin and a new sense of wellbeing.

Running

Running is the most satisfying form of aerobic exercise for many people. No special training is needed and it can be done anywhere—at home or on holiday. All you need is a good pair of running shoes and the self-discipline to get started. You may be surprised to find that before long you too are hooked and can't imagine life without this liberating activity.

Before you start on a programme of running, it is important to check your fitness. If you are over thirty-five, suffer from high blood pressure, have a family history of heart disease or have recently been ill, it is a good idea to have a check-up with your doctor to make sure that running is safe for you.

There is a simple way to check your own fitness level. Simply walk two miles in thirty minutes at a brisk pace and ask yourself how you feel afterwards. If you feel no nausea or dizziness you are fit enough to start a graded programme of running. If, however, you find the two-mile walk difficult, persevere until you can do it comfortably in half an hour. You may be surprised how quickly this happens—walking for half an hour each day can have a marked effect on your condition.

Here is a programme that you can follow:

First Week:

Take a brisk walk of one mile, breaking into a jog of roughly 50–100 metres whenever you feel like it. In between these jogs, walk at a steady pace but do not force yourself. Pushing yourself too hard in the beginning is counter-productive and you could end up with strains or injuries that set you back. You should feel relaxed enough that you are able to appreciate your surroundings.

Second Week:

Walk/jog for a mile, alternating about 100 strides of each at a stretch.

Third Week:

Walk/jog for one and a half miles, increasing your jogging intervals to 150 strides with 100 strides of walking in between.

Fourth Week:

Jog for a while at the speed that you find most comfortable. Don't worry if you have to stop from time to time to walk, although by now you should be finding that minor discomforts are fleeting and that you can run through them.

Fifth Week:

Run a mile in less than nine minutes.

Sixth Week:

Jog/run for one and a half miles or more. By now you should have passed through the initial barrier and be beginning to reap all the rewards of your perseverance. You will be more aware of your body and able to listen to what it is telling you. Your stamina will be increased and you can vary your running by pushing yourself more on the days when you feel in top condition and ready for a challenge.

By the end of six months, you should be able to run easily and steadily for between half an hour and an hour, covering a distance between three and nine miles. This programme leads on to a flexible regime of running. Enjoy running and don't get fixated with rigid training schedules. To reap the true benefits of running, aim to run for thirty minutes at least three times a week. This is more effective at building fitness than one running session of one and a half hours. If you want to run every day, it is a good idea to take one day off each week to give your muscles a chance to restore themselves and build up their store of glucose again. This day of rest will only improve the quality of your running.

Running has knock-on effects for health and relaxation. The more you run, the more you will feel in touch with your body. You will find yourself naturally drawn towards healthier foods, your skin will be clearer, and health problems like constipation and insomnia will disappear. As you look better and feel better, you may feel that running is addictive in the best sense of the word.

What to Wear

Clothes made from fabrics that breathe, like cotton, are much better than those made from man-made fibres. In summer a pair of shorts and a T-shirt are ideal: running in bare legs increases the sense of freedom. In winter a cotton tracksuit with a fleecy lining is fine, perhaps with a lightweight waterproof jacket when it's raining. If it is very cold outside a wool cap will protect your ears.

Proper running shoes are not cheap, but they are an excellent investment. They should be not too flexible, without studs and with a high-density sole. Some excellent soles are made of microcellular rubber. Some soles on running shoes extend up the toe and heel to take account of the rocking movement from heel to toe that comes with running. The padded instep helps to absorb shock from running on hard ground. These special design features make you far less likely to risk the sort of injury to tendons or muscles that can come if you run in an old pair of tennis shoes. There should be plenty of room inside for your toes to move about and the heel should be slightly raised to help prevent injury to your Achilles tendon that comes with overstretching. It should have at least five set of holes for laces, so the shoe hugs your foot: in fact, the shoes should feel, when you are out and running, as if they are part of your feet. Plastic shoes are not a good idea because they make your feet sweat: light leather or nylon is a much better bet.

Cotton socks help absorb shock and, because you can change them every time you run, they keep your shoes fresh.

Warm Up

It is not a good idea to jump straight out of bed and go running. You need to warm up your muscles and get your metabolic rate up first. If you run when your muscles are stiff or cold after a long period of inactivity, you are much more likely to pull a muscle or injure a joint. Simply moving about the house briskly for ten minutes will ease your body into action but, if you have time, it is a good idea to do some warm-up exercises. These will also limber the back of your legs, tighten your tummy muscles and strengthen your ankles—covering the muscle areas that running leaves out. Here are six stretching and firming exercises that many regular runners rely on:

1 For your calf muscles and Achilles tendons: stand a little under a metre from a tree or wall. With your feet flat on the ground, lean into it until the backs of your legs hurt a little. Hold the position for ten seconds and then relax. Repeat six times.

2 For tight hamstrings at the back of your legs: keeping your legs straight, put one heel up on a table at waist level (lower, if you cannot reach that high). Now lower your head down to your knee until you feel the strain. Hold the position for ten seconds, holding on to your leg or foot to steady yourself if you need to. Repeat (with each leg) six times.

3 For lower back and hamstrings: lie on your back, arms at your sides. Keeping your legs straight, bring them up over your head. Now lower them as far as possible above your head—touching the floor if you can. Hold for ten seconds and relax. Repeat six times.

4 For your shin muscles: sit on the edge of a table and hold a weight of about two kilograms on the front part of your foot just behind the toes (a small bucket or old paint tin filled with stones is ideal). Keep them there for a few seconds and then lower. Repeat a few times with each foot.

5 For your quadriceps: sit on the table and hang the weight over the toes of one foot so the bucket or tin is resting on the floor and you are not stretching the knee ligaments. Now straighten your knee, raising the weight. Hold for a few seconds and then lower. Repeat six times with each leg.

6 For tummy muscles: do twenty sit-ups with your knees bent and your feet tucked under a heavy piece of furniture if this helps you keep your balance. Clasp your hands behind your head and keep your chin in, curling your body up from the floor.

If you don't have time to go through this routine before you run, start running very slowly and keep to a slow, steady jog for the first five minutes or so until your muscles start to warm up. This is very important if you want to protect yourself from injury.

Never run after a meal, a hot bath, or when you are feeling really cold.

Cool Down
It is just as important to cool off properly after a run, and your muscles should cool off gradually. A good way of achieving this is by walking for five or ten minutes after every run. This keeps extra blood flowing through the muscles and helps your body to eliminate the waste products of exercise such as lactic acid, which can otherwise make you stiff or sore.

If you like, do some stretching exercises, such as bending over from the hips. You should find that any muscular aches and pains vanish quickly as your body responds to your new regime and works itself into condition.

Problems

Don't worry if you get a stitch while you are running. Stop and walk or jog slowly through it until it passes. As you become fitter, stitches will become fewer. If you find areas of skin becoming irritated where they rub together—between the thighs, for example—apply a little petroleum jelly to the spot.

If you experience a sharp pain in a muscle, you should stop running. You may have torn some fibres and the muscle may harden and swell, which is a sign that it is bleeding inside. Place a cold compress—like a bag of frozen peas—on the area and, if the pain doesn't go away in a couple of days, it is a good idea to see your doctor. Of course, if you experience a sharp pain in your chest, you must stop running at once and seek medical advice.

Progress

When you first start running you will find yourself breathing deeper and faster as your body seeks more oxygen to meet the new demands being made on it. You may feel some stiffness in your chest as your muscles expand to help you to breathe more fully. After some minutes of running, you will probably experience the 'oxygen debt', when your body demands more oxygen than it is able to process efficiently at that moment. It is quite common at this point to feel that you want to stop. Walk slowly for a while, breathing deeply.

You may also find that your joints feel stiff, with your legs as heavy as lead. They are merely letting you know that they are being used in a way that is unusual for them. This is perfectly normal and will pass.

You will find, however, that when you are able to run for between six and ten minutes without having to stop and walk, you will come into your second wind. Suddenly your running is easier and you find yourself breathing more freely, coursing forward in a fresh and unrestricted way. If you are new to running, it will take time to reach this phase but, as you persevere, eventually it will come every time you run.

After several weeks running, when you can run for half an hour or so without stopping, you may experience your 'third wind'. You run until your legs are beginning to feel heavy and you are breathing hard. You are just thinking that you should stop, when your running suddenly changes gear, becoming almost automatic. Your body feels lighter and you feel as if you could run on and on. This kind of euphoria is known as 'runner's high' and is one of the reasons that running is such a good tool for anyone seeking relaxation in the deepest sense of the word. Perceptions are heightened and, as your mind clears, problems are seen in their proper perspective. It doesn't happen during every run, but it is an experience well worth working towards.

If you make running part of your routine, you will find that you gain energy in every area of your life—mental and physical.

Massage

We massage ourselves nearly every day. The natural re-action to reach out and touch a painful part of the body—such as a sprain—forms the basis of massage. The relaxation and healing powers of massage have been well documented over the past 5,000 years. The therapeutic value of applying oils and rubbing parts of the body to lessen pain and prevent illness was recognized among the ancient Mediterranean civilizations. In the East it was normal to visit your physician when healthy, and the art of preventive medicine was widely implemented. In ancient times scented oils were almost always used when giving massages, creating an early form of aromatherapy massage. More recently, reflexology, shiatsu and Swedish massage have gained popularity. The aims of these different techniques are basically the same—to relieve muscular tension, alleviate fatigue and revive energy.

Massage affects the whole body through rhythmically applied pressure. Gentle pulling and stroking movements increase the circulation of the blood and cause the blood vessels to dilate. The stimulation of nerves and blood will also affect the internal organs. The lymph is a milky white liquid that carries waste substances and toxins away from the tissues via the lymphatic system. Inactivity can cause an unhealthy build-up of this substance, and as the circulation of the lymph is largely dependent on muscle contractions, so massage will help speed the lymph's progress through the system. Active people can also benefit from massage as strenuous activity burns up the muscle, producing an increase of waste products in the muscle tissue. Massage will help to balance the system in both cases and can increase oxygen capacity by 10–15 per cent.

By realigning our bodies, massage can go a long way to repairing our generally damaged postures. Inactive lifestyles and sedentary occupations have created a society of people with cramped, stooped and neglected postures. Not only does massage help to coax the spine and its corresponding physiology back into position, it also makes us more aware of our bodies. Relieved of muscle tension, the body feels lighter and can be borne more naturally and with more poise. Used in conjunction with postural therapies such as the Alexander technique (*see* page 229), massage can help achieve a relaxed yet controlled posture.

Many of the benefits of massage come through the healer/patient contact. Our hands are one of the most sensitive parts of our body, and we experience much of our sense of touch through our hands. An experienced masseur is able to use his or her hands to communicate feelings of harmony and relaxation. A practised masseur will also be able to diagnose the patient through touch. He or she can 'listen' to tension and stress through the texture of the skin, knotted muscles and stiff joints. Old and current sprains, congestion and swelling should all be obvious to a good masseur. The actions of massage— the stroking, kneading and pulling—detoxify the body, improving circulation and lymphatic drainage. After tension and weaknesses in the body have been pin- pointed and relieved, the patient is left feeling, relaxed and energized.

Along with the diagnosis element of massage there are great psychological benefits—the enjoyment of touch and of being stroked and caressed by another per- son. During a massage the patient is coaxed from emo- tional and occupational stresses and brought into the in- tense arena of the here and now. The importance of this kind of one-on-one, nonverbal communication can never be underestimated in our increasingly impersonal and detached society.

Basic Techniques

Massage should take place in a comfortably warm room. Use a mid-thigh level table or the floor. You will need a towel and a bottle of oil; vegetable oil will do, but if you wish you can buy a perfumed massage oil from a chemist or health shop, or mix your own using a blend of aromatherapy oils.

Effleurage (stroking)

The movement of effleurage is slow and rhythmical, using the whole hand in an upward direction towards the heart. Light, gliding strokes are used when working away from the heart. Applied lightly, this has a relaxing effect on the nervous system, while stronger pressure has more effect on the blood circulation and nervous system.

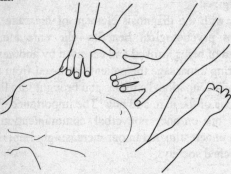

Kneading

Kneading is ideal for unlocking aching or tense muscles, in particular the trapezium muscle between the neck and shoulders. Both hands work together in a rhythmic sequence, alternately picking up and gently squeezing the tense muscle. The kneading gets deep enough to stimulate the lymph into removing the build-up of lactic acid.

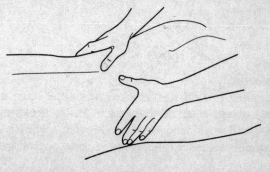

Frictions

Friction strokes are used to penetrate into deep muscle tissue. The heel of the hand, or the tips of the fingers, or the thumb may be used in a linear or circular motion. Thumb pressure is particularly effective for releasing knotted muscle.

Neck and Shoulder Massage

A simple sequence for relieving headaches, loosening the shoulder muscles and providing a general feeling of relaxation.

Neck and Shoulders—A

Stand behind your seated partner. Begin with effleurage, applying firm pressure with both hands. Start at the bottom of the shoulder blades up each side of the spine to the base of the neck. Move your hands apart across the top of the shoulders and then bring them gently down to the starting position. Repeat several times, finishing with a light return stroke.

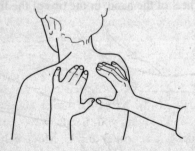

Neck and Shoulders—B

Stand at right angles to the side of your partner. Locate tension points in the shoulders using your thumbs and then work these areas with the thumbs. The pressure can approach your partner's pain threshold but not exceed it.

Neck and Shoulders—C

Place your left hand in an 'L' shape on your partner's shoulder. Applying firm pressure, move it slowly up the whole length of the shoulder. Repeat with your other hand. Continue repeating the sequence using alternate hands. Place one hand at the base of the back of the neck and move it gently up to the hairline, gently squeezing all the time. Return with a gentle stroke. Repeat several times. Without removing your hands, walk round to the other shoulder and repeat B and C. Move behind your partner and repeat A several times.

Back Massage

The following back massage helps to relax the whole body. The strokes should be carried out smoothly, without lifting the hands from the back. Applying thumb pressure to the channels on either side of the spine will help respiratory problems. The same stroke on the lower back can relieve constipation and menstrual discomfort.

Back—A

Place your hands, facing each other, on either side of the base of the spine. Move them up the back, using your body weight to apply pressure. Take your hands round the shoulders and return lightly down the sides of the body. Repeat several times before stopping to knead the shoulders. Work on one shoulder and then the other. Repeat the movement.

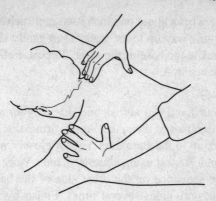

Back—B

Place your hands at waist level, with your thumbs in the hollows on either side of the spine and your fingers open and relaxed. Push your thumbs firmly up the channels for about 5 centimetres (2 inches), relax them, and then

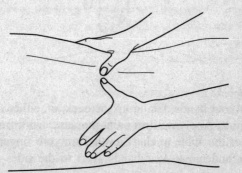

move them back about one inch (two centimetres). Continue in this way up to the neck. Then gently slide both hands back to the base of the spine. Repeat. Follow with the sequence in A.

Back—C

Place your hand flat across one side of your partner's back at the base of the spine. Apply firm palm pressure and work up to the shoulders. Follow closely with your other hand. Repeat using alternate hands. Work through the same sequence on the other side of the back, then repeat on both sides several times. Finish by working through A.

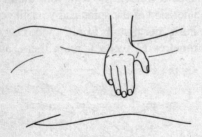

Back—D

Place your hands, facing up the back, on either side of the spine. Applying firm palm pressure, work from the base of the spine to chest level. Turn your fingers outwards and move your hands apart to the sides of the body. Repeat this stroke at waist and hip levels. Repeat the first movement in A several times.

Leg, Foot and Arm Massage
Limbs—A

Begin at the ankle and stroke vertically up the leg with one hand. Follow the same path with your other hand. Continue this sequence, using alternate hands.

Limbs—B

Raise your partner's foot
and hold it with the knee at
a right angle. Using the
palm of your free hand,
stroke firmly down the
back of the leg from ankle
to knee level. Use a light
stroke to return to the ankle. Repeat the whole
movement several times. If
including the foot, work

through D and E next before repeating the whole sequence (A to B) on the other leg.

Limbs—C

Help your partner to turn
over, and begin by stroking
with alternate hands up the
whole leg, as in A. Then put
your hands on either side of
the knee and, using your
thumbs to apply pressure,
circle around the knee cap.
If including the foot, bring
your hands down to the an-

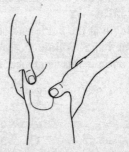

kle and use the sandwich stroke (D) on the front of the
foot. Work through the full movement on the other leg.

Limbs—D

With your partner lying face down, take one foot between your hands, so that the palm of your upper hand is resting in the arch. Press firmly, and slowly draw your hands down to the tip of the foot. Use plenty of pressure for this 'sandwich' stroke.

Limbs—E

Hold the foot with your thumbs lying side by side behind the toes. Pull both thumbs back to the sides of the foot, then push them forward. Repeat this zig-zag movement as you work down to the heel. Then push firmly all the way back to the toes, keeping your thumbs side

by side. Repeat the whole movement several times. Work through the whole sequence (D to E) on the other foot.

Limbs—F

Take hold of your partner's
hand as in a firm hand-
shake, and lift the arm up
slightly, as far as the elbow. Gently place the palm
of your free hand across the
top of the wrist and close
your fingers round the
raised arm. Apply firm pres-

sure and slide your hand up to the elbow, or as far as the
shoulder. Move your palm underneath the arm and use a
light stroke to return to the wrist. Repeat several times.

Limbs—G

Place your thumbs across
the inside of your partner's
wrist. Applying pressure
with both thumbs, make
wide circles around the
wrist area. Repeat F. As
you finish, relax your hold
on the wrist and pull off
firmly and slowly in a
sandwich stroke, as in D.

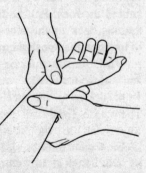

Repeat the full sequence (F to G) on the other arm, finishing with the hand variation of D.

Face and Head Massage

The following sequence encourages deep relaxation. Gentle stroking of the forehead (B) can help to relieve stress-related tension and headaches, while pressure applied to the sides of the nose and along the cheekbones (C) alleviates nasal congestion and sinus problems. Scalp massage (D) stimulates circulation.

Face and Head—A

Use alternate hands to stroke up one side of the face, starting beneath the chin and working up towards the forehead. Do the same on the other side. Repeat several times. Finish by placing one palm across 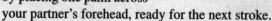 your partner's forehead, ready for the next stroke.

Face and Head—B

Begin by stroking up the forehead with alternate palms. Then place the pads of the middle three fingers of both hands in the centre of the forehead between the eyes. Draw them gently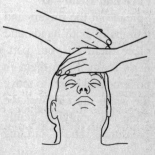

79

apart across the brow and round the outside corners of the eyes. Lift off the middle two fingers and use your fourth fingers only to return under the eyes towards the nose.

Face and Head—C

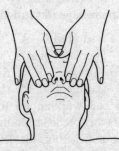

Position your thumbs on your partner's forehead. Using the three middle fingers of both hands, press firmly against the sides of the nose. Continue along the top of the cheekbone, until you reach the temple. Keeping your thumbs in position, return to the nose, pressing along the middle of the cheekbone.

Face and Head—D

Spread out the fingers and thumbs of both hands and place them on your partner's scalp. Keep them in position and begin to move the scalp muscle over the bone by applying gentle pressure and circling slowly and firmly on the spot. Stop occasionally to move to a different area, then begin again, working gradually over the whole scalp.

Acupressure

Acupressure works in a similar way to massage in that it depends on sympathetic personal contact. Like acupuncture, it is based on the premise that our life force permeates to all parts of the body via a system of meridians. Acupressure seeks to balance this flow of energy by stimulation or sedation. The spine, internal organs and the central nervous system are all affected by pressing acupuncture points. Menstrual cramp, headaches, back pain, depression and sleeplessness all respond well to these forms of massage—basically a form of acupuncture using fingertips instead of needles.

Swedish Massage

Swedish massage deals with the soft tissues of the body. It is named after Professor Ling, a 19th-century Swedish academic who carried out valuable research on the technique. It involves several different types of movement: effleurage (stroking), kneading, cupping and hacking. The movement of effleurage is slow and rhythmical, using the whole hand in an upward direction towards the heart. When applied lightly it has a relaxing effect on the nervous system, while deeper pressure has more effect on the blood circulation and nervous system. Kneading is ideal for aching or tense muscles, in particular the trapezium muscle between the neck and shoulders. The kneading gets deep enough to stimulate the lymph into removing the build-up of lactic acid and other waste.

Breathing

'Don't hold your breath' is an often heard expression, and one that suggests that we are always in full control of our breathing. Usually, of course, we are, but that is not always the case.

Breathing is of great value in relaxation. People who are at ease with themselves and the world breathe slowly, deeply and rhythmically. Breathing is the only automatic function that we are capable of controlling. It is carried out partly through the autonomic nervous system and partly through the central nervous system. The autonomic nervous system controls vital functions, endocrine (hormone) secretions and emotions. By controlling our breathing, we can influence all of these and take over conscious responsibility for them.

During a normal day we take between 16,000 and 21,000 breaths. This automatic action is one of the first things to go when we become stressed. Our breathing gets shallower and accelerates erratically. Erratic breathing patterns lead to disorientation and emotional wavering, which can create even more stress—thus a vicious cycle begins. Investigating the breathing pattern and learning to control it is an important step in learning to control stress.

The brain controls our breathing by checking the ratio between oxygen and carbon dioxide in the blood. We exhale when the carbon dioxide makes the blood too acidic. Hyperventilation (fast, deep breathing) makes us expend too much carbon dioxide, leaving the blood in an alkaline state. This induces dizziness and disorientation, as the brain is starved of carbon dioxide.

Habitual hyperventilation causes fainting, numbness, palpitations, sweating and chest aches—all symptoms of carbon dioxide deficiency. These create a cause and effect cycle—erratic breathing induces other unpleasant symptoms, which in turn make our breathing worse.

Obviously, these symptoms occur when we are very stressed. But there are more subtle signs that breathing patterns could be better—gulping, holding the breath, moving the upper chest when talking and breathing, and frequent yawning.

Try a simple test to find out if you are breathing correctly. Lay a hand on the upper section of your chest and the other hand on the lower part of your rib cage. If only your chest moves when you breathe, then you are breathing ineffectively. If the lower edge of the rib cage expands and the stomach rises at the start of each breath, then you are breathing correctly.

When stress hits, regular breathing is the first thing to go. To enable you to maintain easy breathing under stress, it is important to practise breathing exercises. It can sometimes seem difficult to slow down and become conscious about such an automatic act, but regular controlled breathing exercises are a very good way of getting your whole body to relax and to work out stress. Just a few minutes each day given over to fully concentrating on these exercises will bring great relief from stress.

Bad posture can effect the flow of air in and out of the body. Try lying down on your back to give the lungs and diaphragm freedom to move and leave the body relaxed and flexible. By removing the upright strain on your body and lungs there is more chance of developing an easy breathing pattern.

While breathing, focus on raising the abdomen, and filling lower, mid and upper sections with air. Be aware of the expansion of your ribs as you hold your breath—concentrate on that feeling. To exhale, pull in your diaphragm towards the back of your spine, slowly and smoothly. Try to ensure that you fully empty your lungs before inhaling again. This is commonly overlooked when breathing, which means that the lungs are never used to their full potential.

Rhythmic Abdominal Breathing

The following exercises train your body to do what is,

after all, the most natural thing in the world—breathing—in the most effective and relaxing way.

Arrange to have two free periods per day, each of about ten minutes. Find a quiet room where you know you will not be disturbed. Lie down, or sit in a reclining position—try both positions and choose whichever is most comfortable. Rest your hands on your upper abdomen and close your eyes.

The aim is to breathe deeply, slowly and rhythmically. Inhale through your nose—slowly and deeply. Your abdomen should rise gently underneath your hands as the breathing begins. An awareness of this rising and falling of your abdomen is important to establish that your diaphragm is being used properly. Your inhalation should be slow and unforced.

While breathing in, silently and slowly, count three or four as you fill your lungs. When your inhalation is complete, pause for a second or less and slowly start to exhale through your nose. As you do so, you should feel your abdomen slowly descend. Count as you breathe out, and try to ensure that you take at least one count longer (four or five) than when you breathed in. Try gradually to slow and deepen the inhalation phase, and ensure that the exhalation phase lasts at least as long. By concentrating on the exhalation phase, the inhalation phase becomes easier to lengthen.

Remember to start each breath with a rise of the abdomen. The pattern of breathing should be repeated fifteen to twenty times. Once the mechanics and counting have become well established as a pattern, it is useful to introduce a variety of thoughts during different phases of the cycle. For example, on inhalation, try to sense a feeling of warmth and energy entering your body with the air.

On exhaling, sense a feeling of sinking and settling deeper into the support beneath you. A sense of warmth and heaviness accompanying the repetitive breathing cycle will begin the relaxation process. The exercise will slow down the heart rate, reduce sympathetic nervous activity, relax tense muscles and allow a chance for the balancing, restorative, parasympathetic nervous function to operate, as well as calming the mind.

After finishing the exercise, do not get up at once, but rest for a minute or two, enjoying the awareness of feelings of stillness, warmth or heaviness.

Breathing and Repeated Sound Technique

Sit or lie in a comfortable position in a warm, quiet room. Close your eyes and encourage a feeling of heaviness and stillness. Focus your attention on your body, area by area, briefly, in order to assess them for obvious tension. Start with your feet and pass on to your lower legs, thighs, hips, buttocks, abdomen, lower back, chest, shoulders, neck, face, arms and hands. Don't forget your eyes and your jaw muscles. Only spend a few seconds on each area. As the area is visualized, any tension there should be released. If you are not sure if an area is fully relaxed, tense it for a few seconds and then let it go. This brief progressive relaxation prepares you for the following breathing exercise.

Having let go the tension in your body, begin to breathe in and out through your nose.

Passively pay attention to your breathing and, as you breathe out, say silently and slowly to yourself any one-syllable word.

Breathe in and out at a comfortable, unhurried pace. The rhythm should be as natural and unforced as possible.

Don't attempt to control the rhythm or the depth of the breathing, just keep repeating the word as you breathe out. Continue for about ten minutes.

A feeling of stillness and calm should eventually come. Some people quickly feel deeply relaxed and happy. Others have only a gradual sense of feeling less stressed.

Many people expect immediate, dramatic change from an exercise like this. But it is important to know that there is a degree of stress reduction—whether or not you are aware of it—from the outset. If the exercise is carried out as above, positive physiological changes must take place. It is a mistake to give up too soon because benefits often begin before there is any awareness of them.

Short Alternate Nostril Breathing

This simple technique has its origins in yoga.

Place your right thumb against your right nostril, your right index and middle fingers against your forehead, and your right ring finger against your left nostril. (If you wish to use your left hand, reverse all instructions—left thumb on left nostril etc.)

By pressing lightly with your thumb, close the passage of air on the right side of your nose and inhale slowly and deeply up your left nostril.

Pause for a moment between inhaling and exhaling. During this pause, press lightly on the left side of your nose while releasing your thumb pressure on the right. Breathe out down the right side.

Maintain your hand position and breathe in again through the right side.

Once more, between inhaling and exhaling, pause for a moment and reverse the pressure, so that the next exhalation is again through the left nostril. Continue as above.

Achieving Relaxation

This basic technique can be adapted to include counting slowly to three while breathing in, pausing for a count of two, and then breathing out to a count of six.

By focusing on the mechanics and the counting rhythm, a degree of distraction and relief from current problems takes place.

The cycle of alternate breathing can be repeated between five and twenty times. Usually, a sense of peace and relaxation is felt after about seven cycles. This exercise can be a useful escape measure when feelings of stress and anxiety take hold.

Yoga

Originating many thousands of years ago, yoga is the oldest holistic philosophy of living. Its name derives from the same Sanskrit root as the word 'yoke'—hence the system implies the union of physical, mental and spiritual health. Practised regularly, yoga creates mental clarity and emotional stability as well as a sense of deep relaxation and body awareness.

One of the central theories of yoga is the interdependence of all things—animate and inanimate—within the whole universe. It mirrors the fact that we have to look at all aspects of our lives in order to achieve an inner balance and equilibrium. As we are affected by stress from all areas it is vital to address every aspect of our lives and health.

Yoga plays an important role in the practice of Hinduism, but it would be a mistake to regard it as a religion. As it does not require the adherence to any particular dogma, practitioners are free to enjoy its benefits while their own rules of faith remain disparate. It is basically a technique for personal development, enabling people to reach their potential and stretch their spiritual boundaries.

The practice of yoga consists of two main components. These are known as *asanas* (physical postures) and *pranayama* (controlled breathing). The asanas stretch all parts of the body and even massage the internal organs, glands, circulation and respiratory systems. They work by being held for a particular period of time, anything from a few seconds to half an hour. The positions are synchronized with the breathing and affect every part of the body, restoring full flexibility.

Slow, sure and rhythmical, the movements help to loosen the body up. There must never be any sudden jerky movements. Holding onto a position helps strengthen the body at this point, gently pushing it against the movements' limitations. Our inactive lifestyles have resulted in a deterioration of our postures, a stiffening of the joints and premature ageing. Regular yoga can reverse these symptoms.

It is in essence a very balanced philosophy that works all aspects of the body. This will in turn restore a poised and symmetrical posture. The spine especially benefits from yoga, as it is fully exercised, stretched, pushed forwards and backwards and twisted laterally.

The pranayama are intended to relax the body and calm the mind, increase circulation and stimulate the blood supply to all parts of the body. Breathing should be done through the nose, and it is important never to hold a breath. A movement is carried out during an exhalation, with a deep inhalation immediately before it.

Following a basic sequence of asanas is an excellent way of achieving mental clarity and maintaining physical suppleness. Focusing on certain positions can help with particular problems, but it is better to follow a structured sequence of asanas, which will benefit the whole body. This is because the tension in one pose is complemented by the counter-stretch in another.

To experience the full benefits of yoga it is important to practise at least three times a week, leaving plenty of recovery time between sessions. It is also important to relax your body completely before beginning a series of asanas and to wind down slowly afterwards. Yoga is an excellent way of fighting tension and giving a mental and physical boost but it is not something to be rushed into. Look for a class in your area and always seek advice from an experienced tutor before beginning.

The following sequence of asanas gives you an idea of the movements involved, but it is vital to learn the proper movements and holds from a trained yoga teacher.

Before you begin
- Establish a convenient and regular time to practise.
- It is important not to have a full stomach.
- Wear comfortable and loose clothing.
- Use a clean, soft blanket or mat, thick enough to pro-

tect your spine and large enough to fit the length of your body.

• Perform each exercise slowly, carefully and mindfully. Force and strain must be avoided.

Yoga Positions

Cat

Kneel on all fours with your hands shoulder-distance apart and your knees the same distance apart as your hands. Your elbows should remain straight throughout the entire exercise. Exhale while arching your back up high. Keep your head between your arms, looking at your abdomen. Hold this pose for a few seconds. Inhale, as you slowly hollow your back to a concave position. Raise your head and look up. Hold again. Repeat the sequence five to ten times, creating a slow flowing movement of the two postures. Relax.

The Cat helps to strengthen the spine, improve posture and revitalize the whole body.

Tree

Stand with both feet together, arms loosely by your side. Focus your eyes on an imaginary spot directly ahead of you. Bring the right foot up and place the sole against the inside of the left thigh, as high as possible. When balanced, raise both arms simultaneously, placing the palms together over your head. Hold for thirty seconds. Gently lower your arms. Release your foot from your thigh. Repeat the sequence with the other foot. Relax.

The Tree promotes concentration, balance and stability of body and mind.

Triangle

Stand with your feet just less than a metre apart. Inhale and raise your arms sideways to shoulder level. Turn your left foot ninety degrees to the left and your right foot forty-five degrees to the left. Exhale and bend from the waist to touch the left foot with the left hand. The right arm points up, forming a straight line with the left arm. Turn your face towards the upraised hand. Hold for ten seconds. Inhale and return to a standing position. Turn your feet to the right in the same manner and perform the exercise on the right side—slowly, smoothly and carefully. Relax.

The Triangle helps to calm the nerves, acts to remove toxins from the body, and promotes good health in general.

Simple Twist

Sit with outstretched legs. Pull the right leg towards the

body. Place the right foot across the left leg on the floor, next to the left knee. Inhale. Twist the upper body to the right, placing both hands on the right side of the body on the floor. Look over the right shoulder and exhale. Hold for at least ten seconds. Inhale as you slowly move out of the posture and repeat on the other side. Relax. This is a gentle posture that is easy to perform.

The Simple Twist helps to strengthen the spine, improve posture and promote psychological balance and self-confidence.

Cobra

Lie face down. Place the palms on the floor under the shoulders, fingers turned slightly inwards. Slowly lift the forehead, the nose, the chin, and the entire upper body, up to the navel. The weight rests on both hands, the pelvis and the legs. Keep the elbows slightly bent, and do not allow the shoulders to hunch up towards the ears. Hold for ten seconds, focusing your attention on the lower back. Very slowly lower your trunk to the floor, then the chin, the nose, and the forehead. Relax.

The Cobra increases blood supply to the abdominal organs and helps to relieve digestive problems and correct kidney malfunctions.

Plough

Lie on your back, arms by your sides, palms down. Slowly raise your legs and trunk off the floor. Supporting your hips with both hands, bring your legs slightly over your head. Keep your legs as straight as possible. Supporting your back with both hands, continue lifting your legs up and over your head until the toes come to rest on the floor behind your head. Only when you are quite comfortable in the position, release the hold on your back and place your arms flat on the floor. Hold only for ten seconds in the beginning. After your body becomes accustomed to this position, you may hold it longer. Very slowly unroll your body to the starting position. Relax.

The Plough helps to invigorate the entire nervous system, eliminating fatigue, listlessness and exhaustion. It is of particular benefit to the pancreas and endocrine glands.

Forward Bend

Make sure you are well warmed up before attempting this posture. Sit with your legs stretched out in front of you, knees very straight. Inhale and stretch your arms above your head. Exhale and very slowly and smoothly bend forward from the hips (*not from the waist*) to grasp your toes. If at first this seems difficult, clasp instead your ankles, calves or knees. It is important that your legs remain straight. Continue to bend forward and down, aiming to touch your knees with your head. Hold for at least ten seconds and observe your breath. Release your hold and very slowly unroll your spine, returning to a sitting position. Repeat twice.

The Forward Bend slows the respiratory rate to produce a calm and relaxed state of mind. It also increases the suppleness of the spine and improves blood circulation—which helps to regenerate the abdominal organs and improve digestion.

Salute to the Sun

This classic exercise coordinates breathing with variations of six yoga poses in a flowing rhythmic way that stretches and relaxes your body and your mind.

Start by facing east, standing up as straight as you can without forcing it, with your feet together. Inhale and visualize the sun just beginning to rise. Exhale and bring the palms of the hands on to your chest as if you were praying.

Inhale again, stretching your arms overhead as you do so, pushing the pelvis forward a little, and look up at your hands.

Breathe out, bending slowly from your waist until, ideally, your hands are touching the floor in front of or beside your feet. (Don't force this: if you can't reach the floor, let your hands hold on to the lowest part of your legs they can reach.)

Breathe in and lunge forwards by bending your left knee to a right angle and stepping your right foot back. Turn your toes right under and straighten your body from head to heel.

Holding your breath, move the left foot back, toes curled, until you are in the classic push-up position.

Now exhale and drop your knees to the floor, with your bottom up. Bend the elbows and bring your chest and chin to the floor. Continue breathing out and lower the whole body to the floor, straightening your legs and keeping your toes curled under.

Inhale, pushing down on your hands and slowly lifting your head as you straighten the elbows. Arch your back upwards like a snake before it strikes.

Breathe out and, with the buttocks as high in the air as you can raise them and with the head down, form a pyramid.

Breathe in and lunge forward by bending your right knee and stepping your right foot forward between your hands.

When you breathe out, straighten your right leg and bring the left foot next to the right. Lift your buttocks high until you are touching your toes.

Inhale and slowly lift the spine, visualizing it unrolling one vertebra at a time. Raise your head and look up, bringing your arms straight overhead, and bring the image of the rising sun back to mind.

Breathe out and slowly bring your arms back to the sides, allowing the sun to glow brighter and brighter in your mind's eye.

Salute the sun six times at first, gradually increasing the number of repetitions until you are comfortably doing the routine twenty-four times.

Shiatsu

Shiatsu is a Japanese healing art combining the principles of traditional Chinese medicine with practices similar to those of acupuncture but performed without needles. Shiatsu is a balance—a dance—between practitioner and receiver, in which the healing power of both build upon each other to clear and balance the vital force known as *qi*.

Shiatsu is a Japanese word: *shi* meaning finger, and *atsu* meaning pressure. But shiatsu is more than acupressure. It is a combination of many different techniques, including pressing, hooking, sweeping, shaking, rotating, grasping, vibrating, patting, plucking, lifting, pinching, rolling, brushing, and, in one variation—barefoot shiatsu—it includes walking on the person's back, legs and feet.

But these are merely the physical techniques. With an awareness of psychological and spiritual implications, shiatsu has become a kind of dance between giver and receiver. A rapport develops between the practitioner and client, because shiatsu relies on the simple but powerful experience of touch to awaken the client's own self-healing powers. This 'touch communication' is fundamental to all healing methods.

No needles, creams, machines, devices or other para-phernalia are needed for the experience of a complete shiatsu session. The practitioner uses gentleness, fluid-ity and rhythmical motion to work with the imbalances in the client's qi. Progressively, over a number of ses-sions, the client can learn how to assist in the balance of his or her own qi.

Some shiatsu practitioners use a massage table; others use the floor in order to apply a wider variety of tech-niques. If the floor is used, the person lies on a futon, an exercise mat or a mattress especially made for shiatsu. The practitioner then works by kneeling, sitting, crawl-ing and standing near the client. The client remains fully clothed for shiatsu, with loose, comfortable clothing. The body and/or feet may be covered with a sheet or blanket. The room is maintained at a comfortable tem-perature, and soft background music can help to bring the person to a relaxed state of body and mind.

Qi flows through the meridian pathways in all parts of the body. There are more than 300 acupoints along the way. Acupuncture requires the insertion of a single nee-dle for each acu-point selected. In shiatsu the applica-tion to these meridian pathways by the practitioner's fingers, hands, knees or elbows covers several of these critical points simultaneously.

Continual diagnosis is part of the treatment. It is a

supportive system: reciprocal, interdependent, and co-operative between giver and receiver. The healing energy and awareness build in this synergy for both practitioner and client. Throughout this duet in movement, the use of the practitioner's two hands—mother hand and messenger hand—allows continuous motion. The client experiences no pain, but rather a comfortable feeling of partnership in the awakening of powerful self-healing forces. Mutual meditation on the origin of deep breathing clears the mind, allowing fresh oxygen to replenish and rejuvenate the internal organs, so that a deeper sense of self-awareness evolves and healing occurs.

In the practice of shiatsu, each person is primarily responsible for his or her own health and wellbeing. This contrasts with the Western belief that the medical practitioner is principally responsible for our health. In Western medicine, as awareness of the unique significance of touch—the essential form of communication between two human beings in the fight to subdue pain —has almost disappeared; certainly it has become minimal. Ironically, in all times and all cultures, the importance of touch has been acknowledged as a primary means to mitigate pain. In the hurried round of the Western hospital doctors checking hospital charts, this important fact is largely ignored.

Simple Shiatsu Procedures

Sit quietly on the floor, on a cushion. Place one hand on top of the other, over the navel. Clear your mind and concentrate on deep breathing, focusing on a starting point 4 centimetres (1½ inches) below the navel. This point is known as *ki-ka* or 'ocean of energy'. Breathe deeply, and perhaps (to be sure your mind is clear of its daily clutter) you might hum softly as you slowly breathe out. These sounds have a soothing effect.

After a few minutes of deep breathing, lean forward onto your hands as you exhale your humming vibrations. Now inhale slowly as you gently straighten the spine and return to your original sitting position.

Repeat five times.

Now clasp both hands so that they interlock in the Vs between the index finger and thumb. You are touching a major acupoint, large intestine number four, called *go kuku* ('meeting mountains'). Press the thumb, leaning in towards the base of the index finger. Hold the pressure for five seconds, release for five seconds. Repeat for relief from headache, toothache, menstrual cramps, or gastritis.

This simple form of self-shiatsu affects the internal organs. You can increase a specific effect through your focus. For example, when you are bending forward, concentrate on the kidneys in the lumbar area—your lower back. This will strengthen your qi.

Meditation

Through meditation we seek to achieve a state of passive alertness that transcends the everyday level of thought and distraction. Achieving this 'higher level' of consciousness may at first seem a difficult proposition, but with practice and effort it is something all of us can do. Some people are put off by the image of meditation as something steeped in impenetrable Eastern mysticism, but meditators don't have to submerge themselves in religious or spiritual teaching to gain from this art. Meditation is really a very simple way of lightening the mind, forgetting about everyday stresses and concentrating solely on mental relaxation

Although meditation has existed for several thousands of years, it was only during the 1960s that it became popular in Western culture. Today many thousands of people benefit greatly from regularly sitting in a quiet place and focusing their attention on an object for a short period of time. Meditation has several effects on the body. As well as slowing down the heart rate, it can significantly reduce the oxygen consumption and carbon dioxide production of meditators. Within a few minutes of starting to meditate these can fall up to 20 per cent below normal levels. Meditation also raises levels of skin resistance to pain or an electrical current, which tends to fall when we are stressed and anxious. This indicates an increase of muscle relaxation and can account for phenomena such as walking through fire or lying on a bed of nails.

During meditation there is also a reduction of activity in the nervous system. The branch responsible for calming us down, the parasympathetic branch of the autonomic nervous system, dominates. Lactate, manufactured by the metabolism of the skeletal muscles, is also significantly reduced. While meditating, blood lactate models decrease about four times faster than they do when the body is in a normal state of rest. The most likely reason for this decrease is that the blood circulation increases, thereby increasing the delivery of oxygen to the muscles and inhibiting the production of lactate. During meditation the body achieves what is called a hypometabolic state. This is a different state from that experienced during sleep or while under hypnosis and can best be described as deep and prolonged relaxation.

Meditation has also been shown to have a significant effect on the way our brains work. During meditation the brain manufactures a balanced pattern of alpha and theta brain-wave rhythms. Recent research suggests that this may indicate that while in a state of deep relaxation the brain is better able to find a balance between its logical and rational and its creative and imaginative sides. The result of this improved functionality is healthier, more productive and fulfilled individuals. Practised regularly, therefore, meditation helps fight depression, reduce hypertension and relieve anxiety, migraine and psychosomatic illness. Research also shows that concentration, memory and creativity are improved through regular sessions of meditation.

Regular meditation is also of great benefit for those who suffer from low energy and who have difficulty sleeping. The quality of sleep improves when meditation is practised regularly, and most meditators testify to feeling less tired throughout the day, needing less sleep at night and waking up feeling more refreshed. Meditators in training centres in Burma and Thailand can reach the point where they need only four hours of sleep.

When starting to meditate it is important to find a quiet, peaceful area and to use the same place regularly. The familiarity of a sympathetic environment will help you to slide into meditation mode. Soft background music, incense or low lights are the tools some people use to create a conducive atmosphere. Environmental music, featuring the sound of waterfalls, rain or birdsong is proving increasingly popular with meditators. Practised meditators, however, are eventually able to meditate in busy, crowded places such as bus stations and offices.

Try to meditate for around twenty to thirty minutes

each day. There are two stages involved in the process of meditation. First comes physical relaxation, where the focus of attention is on the body and tension build-up is tackled. Once the body is relaxed, the clarifying and emptying of the mind can begin. Given practice, the first stage will become easier to complete and a greater proportion of the time used for meditation can be given to calming the mind.

Some people find it useful to contemplate an object as they meditate. Traditionally, a single flower or a flickering flame is used, but it is entirely up to the individual—whatever concentrates the mind and helps to clear it of clutter—there are no set rules. The visualizing form of meditation can also involve imagining yourself in some peaceful or inspiring setting. Perhaps swimming in a wide blue ocean or moving through a green field; again you are limited only by your imagination. This method can be particularly powerful in banishing negative thought, anxiety or stress.

Posture

Posture is very important in meditation. In Eastern cultures the condition of the body is thought to reflect the health of the mind and spirit, so successful meditation requires that the spine be kept straight. This is thought to assist the channelling of energy from the mind through the body. During meditation you should feel relaxed but not sleepy, and maintaining an upright position helps this. It is not necessary to use one of the Eastern cross-legged postures—lying on your back can be effective—but they are worth mastering. The traditional meditation postures ensure that the body is stable, symmetrical and immobile, and there is also an easy passage for the circulation of blood in the brain, spine and abdomen. The centre of gravity is established below the navel. The Japanese call this area the *tanden*, 'vital centre'.

Many practitioners of the art of yoga consider that the centuries-old seven-point posture is the best for helping to achieve a calm, clear state of mind and has yet to be bettered.

Others recommend the Siddhasana, while many beginners opt for a simple cross-legged position (the easy posture), sitting in a chair (Egyptian posture) or kneeling with the buttocks on the ankles (Japanese posture).

Easy Posture
Basically, this involves sitting cross-legged with both feet on the floor. The back should be straight but not tense and the stomach muscles relaxed. With the muscles of the lower back bearing the weight of the body and with the head, neck and trunk in line, the centre of gravity passes from the base of the spine right through the top of the head. The hands can either rest lightly on the knees or

be held in the lap, either one on top of the other or clasped lightly.

The easy posture

Siddhasana

Sitting on the floor with the back straight, stretch the legs out in front of you. Bend the left knee and, grasping the left foot with both hands, draw it towards the body until the heel is resting against the part of the lower

Siddhasana

body that lies between the anus and the genitalia. Now draw the right foot towards the body until the heel is on the pubic bone. Tuck the toes of the right foot between the calf and the thigh of the left leg. Rest the hands, palms upwards, on the knees. Siddhasana is sometimes called the perfect posture.

Seven-point Posture

1 If possible, try to sit with the legs crossed in the lotus position, or *varja* (*see* page 116), with each foot placed sole upwards on the thigh of the opposite leg. To get into the lotus position, loosen up with the exercises on pages 116–117 and then sit on the floor, legs stretched out in front of you. Now bend the right knee and, grasping the right foot with both hands, place it on top of the left thigh, heel pressing into the abdomen. Repeat the process with the left foot. The soles should be turned up, with both knees on the ground.

If you cannot get into the full lotus position, try the half-lotus. Do the same seven exercises before stretching the legs out in front of you. Bend the left knee and put the left foot beneath the right thigh, as close to the buttock as you can get it. Now bend the right knee and put the right foot, sole up, on top of the left thigh. Keep both knees on the ground and the back straight. When you find that you can maintain this position comfortably throughout the session over a period of four or five weeks, you will be able to start trying the full lotus.

Sitting on a hard cushion will encourage you to keep the back straight and help you to sit for longer without getting irritating pins and needles in the legs and feet.

2 The hands should be held loosely on the lap about a centimetre below the navel, right hand on top of left, palms upwards, fingers aligned. Both hands should be slightly cupped so that the tips of the thumbs meet to form a triangle. The shoulders and arms should be relaxed. Never be tempted to press the arms against the body—they should be held a few centimetres away to allow the air to circulate, which helps prevent feelings of drowsiness.

3 The back must be straight but relaxed. Try to imagine the spinal vertebrae as a pile of two-pence pieces delicately balanced one on top of the other that will crash to the ground if it is disturbed. A straight back encourages the energy to flow freely, and you will be able to meditate for longer and longer periods.

4 Many newcomers to meditation find it easier to concentrate with the eyes fully closed. This is not wrong, but it is better to gaze downwards through slightly open eyes. Closed eyes encourage sleepiness and dreamlike images that get in the way of meditation.

5 The jaw and mouth should both be relaxed, the teeth

slightly apart, the lips lightly together.

6 Keep the tongue touching the palate just behind the upper teeth to reduce the flow of saliva and the need to swallow.

7 Bend the neck forward so that your gaze is directed to the floor in front of you. Don't drop it too low: this encourages sleepiness.

The seven point position keeps the body and mind comfortable and free of tension. Beginners should not expect to be able to adopt it right away; it takes time to master.

The lotus position

Before trying to assume the lotus position, practise these floor exercises, which will loosen the joints involved. Try to maintain a straight back and fixed head position throughout each exercise:

1 Stretch the legs straight out in front of you. Bend your right knee so that you can grasp the right ankle with both hands and put it on the left leg just above the knee so that the right foot is extending beyond the left

leg. Keeping a firm grip on the ankle with the right hand, use the left hand to rotate the foot ten times in one direction and ten times in the other. Repeat the exercise with the left ankle and foot on the right leg.

2 Sitting in the same position as for the first exercise, put the right knee on the left leg as before and with both hands grasping the right ankle, lift it above the leg and shake the foot for twenty seconds. Repeat with the other leg.

3 Place the right foot on the left leg as before. Holding the foot in the left hand and wrapping the right hand around the leg at the ankle, lift the right leg as high as you can and make a large circle with the foot, drawing it close to the body at the top of the circle and pushing it away at the bottom. Repeat ten times before doing the same with the other leg.

4 With the palms of the hands flat on the floor behind and beyond the buttocks, bend the right knee and place the right foot as high up the left thigh as you can comfortably get it with the right knee as close to the ground as possible. Hold this position for a minute and then repeat with the other leg.

5 Supporting the body with the left hand flat on the floor in the same position as for the last exercise, put the right foot as high up the left thigh as possible. Place the right hand on the right knee and gently bounce for a count of ten. Repeat with the left leg.

6 Stretch the legs out in front of you and then slowly bend the knees outwards and draw the soles of the feet together. With the soles touching each other, bring the heels as close to the groin as possible and then, holding the toes with both hands, bounce the knees ten times, keeping them as close to the floor as possible. Hold for a count of ten.

7 Do the same as for the last exercise, but when the heels are as close to the groin as you can get them, put the hands on the knees and press them as far down to the floor as you can. Again, hold for a count of ten.

The Egyptian Posture

This involves sitting on a straight-backed chair. The meditator sits firmly and rocks back and forward slightly until his or her weight finds a point of balance. The hands are cupped on the lap, with the left over the right—if right-handed.

Older people, or those with back problems who are unable to sit on the floor, can sit on a chair or on a low bench and lose themselves in meditation just as effectively as the more supple.

The ideal chair is one specially designed to encourage good posture: the chair is backless and has a slanted seat and knee rest. A straight-backed chair can also be used, in which case sit on the front part of the seat with the feet flat on the floor and the legs slightly apart, the lower legs perpendicular to the floor.

It is not a good idea to meditate while sitting in an armchair or on the edge of a bed as the upholstery encourages you to slouch and become drowsy.

The Egyptian posture

The Japanese Posture

In this posture, also called the thunderbolt posture, the meditator sits on his or her knees, keeping them together. Again the back is kept erect, and the meditator rests on the back of the heels. The palms of the hands are rested on the corresponding thighs or can be cupped in the centre of the lap. Popular in Japan, this position also features heavily in Indian yoga.

Some people find this a convenient and comfortable position for meditation as it is easy to keep the spine straight.

The Japanese posture

Lying Flat

This position is called *shavasanaor*, the corpse position.
Lie flat on the floor on a carpet, blanket or hard mattress. Part the legs a little and let the feet flop to the side.
The arms should be slightly away from the body, hands
on the floor, palms up.

Some teachers encourage their pupils to take up this
position and relax for a short time before assuming one
of the other positions for the meditation session. Relaxing like this prepares the mind for the meditation proper.
When you are in the corpse position, starting with the
toes and working upwards towards the brow, flex each
muscle and shake each joint and then relax it before

moving on to the next. When you have flexed the face muscles, go back to the beginning at the toes and tell each muscle to relax.

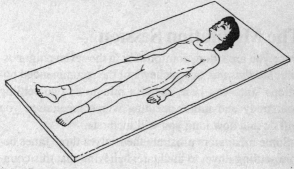

Lying flat

At first, you may feel self-conscious lying on your back saying aloud, 'Toes, relax!', 'Feet, relax!' and so on. But this feeling will soon evaporate when you realize that the method works. When you are completely relaxed, lie still for a few minutes, simply concentrating on your breathing before starting the meditation proper or assuming one of the other positions.

Cupping the Hands

Some teachers recommend that the hands be cupped if the pupil is in a posture where it is appropriate to do so. Right-handed people who decide to do this should cup left hand over the right and, similarly, left-handed pupils should cup the right hand over the left–the aim being to immobilize the dominant hand.

The Meditation Session

Once you are sitting comfortably in the seven point posture, *Siddhasana*, or whichever of the recommended positions suits you best, spend a minute or two settling your body and mind, deciding which meditation you will do and how long you will meditate.

Some meditators prostrate themselves three times before settling down to meditate, believing that this counteracts pride, which is a barrier to effective meditation.

Now run through your thoughts. Set your goals. Why are you about to meditate? What do you hope to achieve by it? The more motivated you are and the clearer your goal, the more successful the meditation is likely to be.

Breathing is central to effective meditation. Breathing well is an excellent way of focusing the mind and blocking out the surface 'chatter' of the mind. In order to achieve this, sit in your chosen position and relax your entire body. Once your eyes are closed, relax and focus on the rhythm of your breathing. It will probably be shallower and slower than usual at first. Slowly deepen your intake of air and watch your stomach rise and fall with each breath. Count each one, saying to yourself 'in' with each inhalation and 'out' with each exhalation. Don't try to push the pace; let it emerge naturally. Slowly you will find yourself focusing entirely on your own breathing. In time this should help to banish other thoughts from your mind.

Many people take up meditation simply to relax, but the more experienced they become, the more far-reaching are their aims, and they feel themselves drawn to the more mystical side of meditation—the search for an understanding of the nature of reality. The deeper they search, the calmer, happier and more satisfied they become. Of course some go too far—assuming a smug, self-satisfied attitude that is not just off-putting to others but defeats the whole object of the exercise.

Which Technique?

There are many different methods of meditation. Some have been handed down from generation to generation for thousands of years and remain in their pure form. Others have been adapted to suit current circumstances. Deciding which of them is right for you can be quite bewildering, but bear in mind that the techniques are not ends in themselves, they are the motorway on which the journey to meditation moves. The best technique for you is the one with which you feel most comfortable.

Experiment

Start, perhaps, with breath-awareness techniques, which are the simplest. Many people go no further. Others experiment with different techniques until they find another method they prefer or they come back to breath awareness. Despite the extravagant claims made by the followers of their own particular favourite, there is no technique that is better than any of the others.

Try not to decide on a method after just one session. Give it a trial run over a week or two, jotting down the frame of mind you were in before you went into meditation and how you felt when you came out of it. At the end of the trial period, try and see if that particular method has improved the quality of your life. If it has, and you feel comfortable with it, stick to it, for by using a method that suits you and making it part of your life you will make faster progress than if you dabble in one and then move on to another just for experiment's sake.

Proper Breathing

This is vital to proper meditation. Generally, you should breathe in at your normal rate through the nose. Don't be tempted to force yourself to breathe more deeply or more slowly than usual. You will probably find that the deeper you meditate, the slower and more deeply you will breathe.

A technique called bellows breathing, or *bhastrika*

pranayama, is recommended by experienced meditators to quieten the mind before meditation proper begins. The practice involves breathing in and out rapidly by forcing the abdominal muscles to expand and contract rapidly. It takes a great deal of practice to breathe properly in this way, and even those who have mastered the technique should never try it until at least three hours after eating, and should eat nothing for at least half an hour afterwards.

It should be noted that breathing in this way can produce dizziness and nausea and should never be practised by pregnant women, anyone with hyper- or hypo-tension or with heart or lung problems. It is best learned from a teacher than from the pages of a book.

The Time . . .

There are no set rules as to how often you should meditate—some people meditate every day, others find just once a week suits them. It doesn't matter as long as you meditate regularly, but remember that if you let too long a period elapse between sessions you will be as out of shape, meditatively speaking, as ballet dancers would be if they didn't go to a class regularly.

There will certainly be days when you are due to meditate when it is the last thing you want to do, but try anyway, even if only for a few minutes. It is best not to meditate for at least two hours after eating a meal.

. . . and the Place

Set aside a corner of a suitable room. Put a mat on the floor and make sure the area is as clean, quiet and pleasing to you as you can make it so that it is a place you will look forward to being in. Make sure, too, that you tell your family you don't want to be disturbed while you are meditating.

Some people burn candles and incense sticks. If you think they will help make the space more conducive to meditation by all means try this. Remember that to meditate effectively you must be as relaxed as possible.

The Meditation Object

This is something on which the attention can focus and on which it may rest, ideally for the full session, although in practice this rarely happens as even experienced meditators may find their attention wandering at some time or other (see below), but the meditation object is always there to come back to.

The object may be something to look at—a flower, a candle, a religious icon or a *mandala* or *yantra*, symbols specially designed for meditation (*see* problems below). It may be something you can listen to, perhaps a cassette recording of the sound of the sea or a running river or birdsong. It can be as everyday as the ticking of the clock or as esoteric as the tinkling of temple bells.

Many meditators use a *mantra*, a word or phrase repeated again and again either out loud or mentally.

The meditation object can even be your own breath.

Problems

Even the most practised meditators may experience difficulties, so beginners should not be put off if they find it hard to get into a meditative state of mind or to maintain concentration.

One of the most common problems is mental excitement. The mind becomes restless and the attention is continually distracted. Sometimes we are unable to banish nagging problems from our thoughts—for example, job security, paying household bills, health worries. If we are in a particularly good frame of mind, we may unintentionally recall things that have made us smile—a new friendship, an enjoyable conversation, even a television programme we have enjoyed.

In our everyday lives we let our minds jump from thought to thought, from worry to worry, so mental wandering is a deeply ingrained habit and, like any habit, is difficult to give up. One popular way of overcoming it is to concentrate on breathing, which has a very calming effect on one's state of mind.

Be patient. It takes time and constant practice to learn how to slow down and control the mind. Don't give up. Even an experienced meditator such as St Teresa of Avila experienced difficulties. When she overheard a novice at her convent remark that it must be wonderful to be 'like Sister Teresa' and not be bothered by distractions during her prayers and meditations, she surprised the girl by saying, 'What do you think I am, a saint?'

Another common problem is drowsiness. When we are in a completely relaxed frame of mind, it is all too easy to drop off to sleep. If you start to feel sleepy when meditating, make sure that you are sitting up straight and your head is not bent too far forward. If you are meditating with your eyes closed, open them and meditate with the gaze directed at the floor in front of you. Turn down the central heating or open a window to freshen the air. Increasing the amount of light in the room can also help you stay awake.

Physical Tension

Any physical discomfort makes effective meditation difficult. Often such discomfort is a physical manifestation of mental turmoil—it could be an unresolved problem or worry, or something that has made you angry. If your meditation is disrupted by physical discomfort for no obvious reason, then try to recognize any such problems and settle them in meditation.

One way of getting rid of physical tension is to focus your attention for a moment on each part of the body in turn, tense it, and then relax it.

Deep, slow breathing can also help. Concentrate as

hard as you can and, as you breathe out, try to imagine the pain or tension evaporating.

Long-term Benefits

Try not to expect too much too quickly. Don't think that because you have been meditating every day for a week or two and feel no benefit, meditation is not working for you. It can take months, sometimes years, for positive changes to show themselves, and even when they do, they can happen over such an extended period you may not be aware of the difference the practice is making to you. Others, however, will certainly realize that something about you has changed for the better.

Breaking the Spell

Avoid coming out of meditation too quickly, for if you do most of the benefits you have achieved will be lost. Once you have finished meditating, remain in your position for a minute or two and then slowly stretch, catlike, quietly reflecting on how good you feel—calmer and better equipped to cope with everyday living. Instead of acting impulsively or emotionally, you will be calmer and able to deal with life's problems in a more relaxed and measured way.

Breathing Meditations

Awareness of Breath

Correct abdominal breathing lies at the heart of all kinds of meditation. In 'awareness of breath' meditation, breathing itself is the object of the meditation. Such meditation is held in the highest regard among Buddhists, Hindus and Taoists, all of whom believe it is not just a means of inducing peace of mind but also of encouraging physical and mental health.

Breathing awareness can also be used as a prelude to another form of meditation. If this is to be the case, five minutes or so will calm the nerves and focus and still the mind, putting it in a receptive mood for the session proper.

Awareness of breath meditation techniques are ideal for the novice meditator because they are entirely natural and most people feel quite comfortable with them. The techniques simply involve being aware of the breath as it enters and leaves the body.

Sit motionless in any of the positions you find comfortable, remembering to keep the back, head and neck in perfect balance, and begin to think about your breathing, becoming aware of each intake of breath, the pause, the expulsion of stale air from the lungs, the pause, the next breath. Your attention will wander. Don't be put off; bring it back to the object of your meditation and start again on the next inhalation.

It is not unusual for the pattern of breathing to change during meditation. At first, when you may be feeling a little self-conscious, you may find that you are holding each breath for longer than usual, but as the meditation proceeds you should find that breathing becomes smoother and deeper, or it may become shallow and slow. Don't be concerned by this. As you concentrate on your breathing and lose yourself in the meditation, the body establishes a rate of breathing that is right for that particular time.

There are several methods for encouraging attention to focus on the breath. None of them is better than any of the others. Try them all and stick with the one you feel happiest with. Naturally they all require you to adopt a suitable posture and choose an appropriate place. One newcomer to breath awareness meditation decided to try it in a stuffy underground train. He closed his eyes, put his thoughts in order, began to breathe in and out as he had learned . . . and was woken by the guard when the train reached the terminus, many stops past his own.

The Simplest Methods
Take up a comfortable posture. You may shut your eyes to aid concentration, but it is better to keep them half open. Breathe as naturally as you can, counting either

each inhalation or exhalation up to ten, and repeat this for twenty minutes. Counting is an aid to concentration and helps to prevent the mind from wandering.

Some people find it helps if they focus their attention on the tip of the nose or the inside of the nostrils as the breath enters and leaves the body. Others use the movement of the abdomen as the focus of their attention.

Mindfulness of Breathing Meditation

'A monk having gone to the forest, to the foot of a tree, or to an empty place, sits down cross-legged, keeps his body erect and his mindfulness alert. Just mindful he breathes in and mindful he breathes out.' Thus did the Suddha advocate to his followers mindfulness of breathing meditation, also called 'following the breath'.

According to this widely practised method of meditation, the abdomen or nose is the focus of attention.

There is no counting in mindfulness of breathing meditation, rather it is the flow of breath in and out on which the mind is concentrated. To practise it, sit comfortably in any of the prescribed positions with the eyes closed and breathe in and out quite naturally, focusing the attention either on the abdomen or the nose.

If it's the abdomen, become aware of the pause in breathing at the limit of each sea-swell-like rise and fall of the abdomen. If it's the nose, concentrate on the nostrils where the flow of inhaled and exhaled air can be felt.

You are certain to find at first that your attention wanders, even if you have been successfully practising counting the breath meditation for some time. When you realize that your attention has meandered, simply return it to the abdomen or nose and continue the meditation.

As you give in to the seductive rhythm of your abdomen as it rises and falls or the sensation of the inflow and outflow of air in your nostrils, your breathing will become smoother and quieter as the meditation deepens.

Try to avoid controlling your breathing in any way. This can be difficult. Watching the breath without trying to interfere with it seems simple, but it takes some practice for the mind to become used to the fact that you are trying to surrender yourself completely to the spontaneous flow of the breath. Beginners usually find their breathing becomes uneven, quickening and slowing for no apparent reason. They should not worry, for in time the breath settles to its own rhythm.

Many of those who practise following the breath meditation find it helps if they make themselves aware of the journey of each breath from the moment it enters the nostril to the moment it is expelled. Others picture an aura of energy and light just in front of the forehead. With each breath some of the power is taken into the body and the meditator focuses on the journey deep into the body.

Most of the faiths or religions that advocate breathing meditation have their own techniques. Zen Buddhists, for example, sometimes imagine that a ball of lead drops slowly through the body with each breath making the stale deoxygenized air fall out.

Many have their own methods of dealing with the inevitable distractions. Some Buddhist teachers encourage their pupils to use the distractions themselves as the objects of meditation for a moment before they are dissolved and following the breath can be resumed.

Active Meditation

The Sufi Circle

Most meditations are done on one's own or with a teacher. Movement meditation as practised by some Sufis (best known for their dramatic whirling dancing) is done by groups of five to fifteen people and involves chanting as well.

Form a circle with your companions, standing with feet apart some distance from each other but not so far that you have to stretch your arms as you join hands. Now, very slowly lean backwards raising your face to the ceiling (or sky if you are doing this outdoors) and bring the hands up. When everyone is comfortably looking as straight up as they can, say the words 'Ya Hai' loudly in unison. Now all the people in the group bring their arms down and their heads and bodies forward, until they are facing downwards. Now say, in the same ringing, triumphant tone, 'Ya Huk', and return to the 'Ya Hai' position and repeat again and again, establishing a speed and a rhythm comfortable to everyone in the group. Seen from above, the group would look like a blossom opening and closing in perfect harmony.

The point of this meditation is total involvement of awareness of the movement and the accompanying sounds, and each person must be conscious of the physical condition of each of the others in the group. If someone finds that he or she is having to push himself or herself to keep up with the group as it establishes its rhythm, that person steps back and brings the hands of the people on either side together so that the circle remains intact. There must be complete freedom to do this. No one should feel compelled to keep up: if so, the whole point of the meditation is lost.

The aim is to go beyond fatigue to the point where exhaustion is forgotten and all are so lost in the movement and the chanting that they become unaware of everything apart from the awareness of self and universe being in total harmony—which is the point of all meditation.

Sensory awareness meditation

Movement is also a part of this sensory awareness meditation in which it is combined with breathing awareness.

Begin by lying on your back on a rug or mat. Your legs can be fully extended or drawn in towards the buttocks with the feet flat on the floor. When you are comfortable, close your eyes and concentrate for a few minutes on letting each part of your body in turn sink more deeply into the floor, starting with the feet and moving upwards through the calves, knees, thighs, pelvis, rib cage, chest, hands, lower arms, elbows, upper arms and neck to the head. Concentrate not just on the surfaces that are in contact with the floor but with the sides and top of your body as well.

Now, concentrating on each exhalation of breath, try to feel your whole body sinking deeply into the floor.

After about fifteen minutes, lay your hands on your diaphragm, keeping the upper arms and elbows firmly on the floor. After the diaphragm has moved the hands up and down, up and down for a minute or two, they will feel as if they have been incorporated into the breathing process. Very slowly, raise them a little from the body, concentrating all the time on your breathing, then return them to the diaphragm, allowing them once again to become part of the breathing process.

Repeat this for ten minutes or so, gradually increasing the distance the hands are moved away from the body each time until they eventually come to land on the floor. Slowly you will come to think that the whole cycle is happening by itself with absolutely no effort on your part, and you will find yourself at one with the world.

Tai Chi Ch'uan

Although it is not meditation in the accepted meaning of the word, the aim of Tai Chi (the 'Ch'uan' is usually dropped) is to combine motion, unity and dance so that those who practise its art surrender to the natural flow of the universe and become one with it—exactly the aim of more passive meditation.

Tai Chi is a means of exploring the processes of mind and body through creative movement and reflects the I Ching belief that nature is always in motion. It is said to have originated with the meditation of a Taoist monk, Chang San-feng, who one day saw a magpie trying to attack a snake. The reptile teased the bird by writhing and curling in a spiral motion, always remaining just out of the bird's reach. Similar movements are now an integral part of Tai Chi.

In Tai Chi, the image of water symbolizes the flow of energy. It represents the way the flow of energy yields to the form of its container. Earth is seen as a link between person and planet. The use of circular forms of expression shows unity and containment.

It is not possible to learn Tai Chi from the pages of a book. Traditionally the practice was handed down from master to pupil. Today most large towns offer Tai Chi classes, and anyone wishing to learn its ways and mysteries should join a group.

The classes always begin with a period of meditative stillness, and then the pupils step forward on the right foot—an energy step with fire being visualized shooting from the palms of the hands. Then the energy is pulled back into the body and the weight transferred to the left foot, everyone now visualizing water cascading over him or her. With the body turning to the left, the palms are rotated and curved back to the right. The body continues to turn to the right with both feet firmly fixed to the floor, then the left foot is brought round, returning the body to the centre.

Tai Chi is a process of self-discovery and like yoga demonstrates the link between body, movement and posture, and contemplative states of being. In the words of one expert, Al Huang, who wrote the classic *Embrace Tiger, Return to Mountain*, 'Tai Chi is to help you get acquainted with your own sense of personal growth, the creative process of just being you.'

Attention to Life Meditation

This is not meditation in the strictest sense of the word, and it is not a method to be used in daily or twice-daily sessions. Rather, it is part of everyday activity, its aim being to focus consciously all your attention on the particular movement, activity or task you are performing, to the exclusion of everything else.

Take something as mundane as dishwashing. As you wash each dish, close your eyes and concentrate on feeling each sensation—the warmth of the water, the texture of the plate, the soapiness of the lather, the smell of the detergent. Focus on each part of the activity. To do so, consciously relax all the muscles not essential to the task and work the muscles being used as sparingly as possible.

In focusing your thinking on the task in hand in as concentrated a manner as possible, you are actually meditating, albeit for a very short time, but it is surprising how effective such short-span meditation can be, especially in helping to remove feelings of stress.

Meditation on the Run

Many long-distance runners hit a point, usually about three-quarters of an hour into a run, when they experience what is commonly known as a 'high'. This is remarkably similar to what happens during mantra or chanting meditation, with the rhythmic repetition of the word or phrase being replaced by the rhythm of the run. The runner's conscious mind shuts down, allowing other areas of consciousness to open up.

So, if you enjoy a jog, use it not just to make your body fit, but to put your mind in better shape too.

Don't try to compete with other runners in the park or against the clock to beat your own personal best time. If you do, you are shutting your mind to the possibility of meditation.

Run easily, establishing a regular rhythm, and focus your attention on your breathing, your pulse and heart-beat, and after a while you will reach a point where you will be as perfectly in tune with the world as a Buddhist monk sitting hour after hour in contemplative meditation.

See also Running, page 55.

Mantra

Repeating a word or phrase—a mantra—over and over again is probably the most practised and widespread path to meditation and one of the oldest. Mantra yoga is mentioned in the *Vedas,* the oldest of the world's scriptures. The mantra may be chanted aloud or repeated silently. The repetition of the mantra is known in India as *japa*, and according to the traditions of that country, there are fourteen different kinds of *japa*. Today, in the West, only two of them are in common use—voiced repetition and mental repetition.

The power of the mantra is the power of sound to affect people and alter their state of mind. If you doubt that sound can do this, pause for a moment and consider how irritated you get if someone is playing music too loudly or if you are sitting next to someone who is plugged into a personal stereo and the music is almost audible to you. If sound can irritate, then surely the converse is true—sound can make you feel tranquil, and to focus on a mantra during meditation can lead to some of the deepest and most profound sessions you are likely to experience.

Sound is energy produced by a vibrating object. It is transmitted by waves of different frequencies. Followers of mantra meditation believe that different sounds resonate with different energy centres in the body and that these sounds can be combined in the form of the mantra.

Most of the major religions have their own mantra, as in the Hindu *Hare Krishna*: Hail to Krishna. For those who wish to use a mantra in their religion but who want to avoid religion, any word or phrase, no matter how meaningless, will do.

In India, until the 11th century, it was usual for gurus

to devise personal mantras for each of their pupils. Each pupil treasured this mantra and refused to divulge it to his fellows for he had been warned that in doing so the power of the mantra would be weakened. In the 11th century, Ramanuja, a leading figure in the history of Indian yoga and one suspicious of the almost mystical power of the gurus, shouted his mantra from the roof of a temple so that all could share it. The practice of secret mantras now only survives, generally speaking, in the school of Transcendental Meditation (TM) practised by the Maharishi Mahesh.

Those who are suspicious of any religious aspects associated with mantra can do little better than choose their mantra by the method recommended by Lawrence LeShant, a leading expert on the subject. He advocates the 'La-de' method of mantra selection: simply opening a telephone directory at random and blindly letting the forefinger fall on the page. The first syllable of that name becomes the first syllable of the mantra. Repeat the process, linking the second syllable selected at random with the first and—hey presto!—you have a mantra.

To practise meditation with a mantra, begin, as usual, by taking up the position that you find most comfortable and breathe gently and rhythmically through the nostrils, taking the breath deep into the abdomen. Then repeat the mantra, either aloud or silently, focusing your concentration on it as completely as you can. When your mind has become still, it is no longer necessary to continue repeating the mantra, but, as with other forms of meditation, when you become aware that your thoughts have wandered, start repeating the mantra again, concentrating your conscious thoughts on it.

Once you have chosen a mantra with which you are comfortable, stick with it. It's amazing how in times of stress repeating your mantra a few times silently to yourself restores calm and helps you to put things into proper perspective.

Many mantra meditators repeat the mantra in rhythm with their breathing, saying it once or twice on inhalation and once or twice on breathing out. They are usually repeated silently, but some teachers encourage their pupils to say them aloud, especially if they are leading a group meditation.

Om

Om, a Sanskrit word pronounced to rhyme with 'Rome', is one of the most widely used mantras. According to Hindu belief, *om* is the primal sound and it is accorded the highest value as an object of meditation and is one well worth trying. Breathe in gently, and as you exhale, recite the word as three sounds: 'a' (as in father), 'oo' (as in room) and 'mmm'. Try to feel the sounds vibrating in your body. The 'a' will feel as if it is ringing in your belly, the 'oo' will resonate in your chest and the 'mmm' will positively resound in the bones of your skull. Link the sounds to your breathing rhythm, keeping it slow and calm and avoiding deepening it in any way.

After saying *om* aloud for ten breaths, soften the voice until you are saying the word under your breath, then lower it even further, keeping your attention firmly focused on it. It won't be long until your lips stop moving and the syllables lose their shape, leaving you with just an idea that clings to your mind. Banish any intrusive thoughts by imagining them as puffs of smoke and watch them being blown away by a gentle breeze.

The Jesus Prayer

Some Christians use the name of Jesus as their mantra, others use short prayers, one of the most popular of which is the Jesus prayer, which was probably devised by orthodox monks. It has two forms: either 'Lord Jesus Christ, son of God, have mercy on me', or 'Lord Jesus Christ, have mercy on me'. The prayer follows the advice of a 7th-century mystic who is reputed to have written: 'If many words are used in prayer, all sorts of distracting pictures hover in the mind, but worship is lost. If little is said . . . the mind remains concentrated.' His words could be paraphrased to define mantra—a few words to concentrate the mind.

Humming like a Bee

While not a mantra in the true sense of the word, there are many people who hum while meditating. If you would like to try this, take up your usual position but close your right nostril with your right thumb and inhale through the left nostril, holding your breath as deep and as low in the abdomen as you can. Now exhale and as you do so make a humming noise deep in your throat, focusing your thoughts on the sound.

Do this five times and repeat the exercise with the right nostril, then alternate five times with each nostril for a full twenty-five minute meditation.

Other Techniques to Try

Tactile Meditation

Before you begin, choose an object to hold while you are meditating—something light, for if it is too heavy its weight will affect your concentration and hence your focus. It need not be soft, but it should not be sharp. Now close your eyes and concentrate on the texture of the object in your hand, focusing on how it feels rather than what it is.

Another method of using touch to help reach the meditative state requires a set of worry beads or four or five pebbles. Relax in your favourite position, holding the beads or pebbles in the open palm of one hand and with the other move them rhythmically and methodically between your fingers, counting them one at a time.

Feel each bead or pebble as you count, focusing all your attention on the slow, repetitive movement.

Music and Meditation

The relevance of music as an aid to meditation is a personal one. Its effect depends on facilitating your meditations, and that in turn depends on your own instincts and intuitions.

Percussion instruments have long been used in meditation, especially when it is practised by atavists. The music they produce symbolizes rhythm and vitality.

Gongs and bells are used to purify the surrounding atmosphere, making it more conducive to meditation. Many religions use peals of bells to help their adherents re-gather wandering thoughts. If you want to use bells as an aid, focus your thoughts on the sound, trying to experience it beyond audibility.

Harps have long been associated with meditation. In China the cheng and other zither-like instruments are widely used, and in India the sitar and the vina accompany meditative chanting.

The gentle tinkling of the Aeolian harp can create a perfectly calm state of mind as you approach your meditations, and help you to focus your thought.

To meditate to music, take up your usual position,

close your eyes and listen to a favourite piece, immersing yourself in it completely. Try to become one with the sound, letting it encompass you, and if your thoughts are invaded by thoughts associated with the piece you have chosen, imagine them as musical notes floating off into the distance.

Zen Meditation

The word 'Zen' derives from the Sanskrit *dhyana*, meaning 'meditation'. With its roots in the Yisuddhimagga tradition, it is widely practised in Japan, having arrived there through the Ch'an meditation school of China.

Zen's main practice is *zazen*, or sitting on a cushion facing a wall, and is done daily by those who practise it, usually adopting the full lotus position. Meditation sessions are quite lengthy, hence, in zazen, great stress is placed on correct posture. The body is held upright, and it should theoretically be possible to draw a line from the centre of the forehead down through the nose, chin, throat, navel into the coccyx at the tail of the spine. Every part of the body must be in balance: if it is not, incorrect balance in one part of the body will cause strain in another and ruin the meditation.

The left hand rests within the right, the middle joints of the middle fingers touching, with the thumbs also lightly touching each other, held at the navel, with the arms slightly away from the rest of the body.

Apart from the fact that novices to Zen are sometimes advised to count their breaths from one to ten, and the use of *koan* (*see* below), zazen uses no mantra, mandala or other object of meditation. In zazen, thoughts are allowed to come and go without being banished by the meditator, who remains attentive and alert throughout the meditation, concentrating on sitting as still as possible in a state of quiet awareness.

Zen masters often ask their pupils impenetrable questions, known as koan: an unanswerable puzzle designed to precipitate awakening by breaking through the limited confines of consciousness. A common one is 'What was your face before you were born?' From then on, whenever the koan comes to mind, the pupil banishes all other thoughts and concentrates on his koan. As he comes to realize that there in no answer *per se*, he reaches a state that has been described by those who have achieved it as 'feverish concentration', from which arises 'supreme frustration', and—with conscious thought transcended—the pupil attains *samadhi*, the state of total concentration.

The first koan is said to have arisen when the great Zen master Hui-neng was attacked by robbers. He begged them to be silent for a moment and then said to them, "When you are thinking of neither good nor evil, what is at that moment your original face?" The robbers were so astonished that they begged Hui for an explanation. The master sent them on their way, and the men found that the question came to dominate their thoughts to such an extent that when something else came to mind, they banished it and resumed their meditation on the question, until they found they had arrived at samadhi.

Transcendental Meditation

This form of mantra meditation was introduced to the West in 1959 by the Maharishi Mahesh and became popular in the 1960s when several influential young men and women, including the Beatles, claiming they were disillusioned with Western values, turned to the East for spiritual fulfilment.

Its central feature is contemplation on and repetition of a Sanskrit mantra personally bestowed on each follower by his or her guru, originally Mahesh himself.

In the Maharishi's own words, in TM '. . . the attention comes from outside to the inside, to the source of thought, and then the conscious mind . . . gains that transcendent pure awareness which is bliss consciousness. It is just thinking, but thinking in a manner so that awareness goes deep within and gains that inner being of pure consciousness.'

Those who follow TM meditate for forty minutes a day in two periods of twenty minutes, repeating their mantra inwardly without moving their lips. The two periods of meditation must be separated by at least six hours of normal activity. Unlike many other schools of Indian meditation, TM demands no conscious changes in lifestyle. The Maharishi claims that changes will happen spontaneously as the meditation sessions progress.

A great deal of research was conducted on TM, and it emerged that it did create significant psychological changes associated with relaxation. Sceptics, however, queried the methodology of much of the research, and their constant barracking weakened the validity of some of the findings.

Those who follow TM insist on the mantra being chosen with much ceremony and in secrecy by the master teacher, but this practice has not been shown to be any more effective than one that uses simple words.

Visual Meditation

Visual meditation uses our natural capacity to think in pictures and our ability to create images in what is often called the mind's eye. It may be practised with the eyes open or shut or by opening and shutting them for alternate periods, concentrating on the after-image that remains in our mind when the eyes are closed. The latter is usually recommended for beginners.

Place the object of your meditation (see opposite) at eye level between a metre and two metres from your face. If you decide to use a mandala or yantra (see below) the central point should be level with the eyes. Assume whichever meditation position you favour, and in as relaxed a way as possible, gaze at the image, focusing your attention on it, trying to become *absorbed* in what you are looking at rather than just thinking about it. After two or three minutes, or as soon as you feel any sign of eye strain, close your eyes and visualize the object for as long as you can, still trying to be part of it. Open the eyes again and continue alternating open-eyed and closed-eyed meditation for the full session.

Initially it will be difficult to retain the image in your mind's eye for long when your eyes are closed: don't worry. When the image starts to fade, open the eyes and gaze at the object again. As you become more practised in the art, you will find that you can retain the image for longer and longer.

Meditating on a Candle

One method recommended for beginners is to light a candle in a darkened room—draught-free so that the candle burns as steadily as possible. Sit as motionless as you can in your favourite position and gaze at the flame so that it holds your attention completely. Let the image fill your mind for a minute before closing your eyes. Notice how the candle has imprinted itself on the darkness. Hold it in your mind's eye, not worrying about any change of colour. If it slips to the side, bring it back to the centre and keep concentrating until the image fades completely. Now open the eyes and resume gazing at the candle. Continue in this way for ten minutes at first, gradually increasing the time until you can sit comfortably for a full twenty minutes.

A Flower or a Bowl

Some people begin their visualizing techniques with a flower.

One expert tells his novice pupils to gaze at a patterned china bowl, taking it all in at first, then allowing the eyes to travel over it, tracing its lines and colours, the pattern that decorates it, the way it catches the light. Only when his pupils come to experience the bowl's visual qualities for the first time, does he move on to telling them to close their eyes and try to focus on the image of the bowl held in the mind.

Yantras and Mandalas

To scholars of Sanskrit, *yantra* is a word meaning 'instrument' and *mandala* is a word that means 'circle'—the supreme universal symbol. To the meditator, a yantra is a diagram that possesses the power to transform the consciousness of those who have been introduced to knowledge of what the yantras represent.

A mandala is essentially a type of yantra, the yantra being more specific to a particular deity, the mandala being more general. Both are diagrammatic in form, designed so that the focus of the meditator comes to rest on a central focal point, the *bindu*, which is said to represent the essence of being.

They can be astonishingly beautiful to look at, especially those of Tibetan Tantric Buddhists whose richly symbolic and gloriously designed mandalas have come to be prized by collectors as works of art.

The lotus blossom, the symbol of enlightenment, is widely used as part of the patterns, symbolizing the un-

This is an example of a mandala.

folding of creation. According to Hindu mythology, Brahma stood at the centre of a thousand-petalled lotus before creating the universe, and Buddhists believe that at the birth of the Buddha, a large lotus sprang from the earth and Buddha stepped into its centre. From there he gazed into the ten directions of space: once along each of the eight petals, once upwards and once downwards.

Mandalas and yantras may be drawn, painted or carved in stone. Some eastern mystics meditate on yantras that they draw for themselves in the sand or earth. Such temporary ones often serve as teaching aids between master and pupils.

Meditating with a Mandala or Yantra

Before you can meditate with a mandala or yantra you will have to be instructed on its meaning. Then, place it so that the central point is at eye level when you are sitting before it in your usual meditating position. Relax the muscles of your face and sit absolutely motionless, gazing at the centre point. Let your gaze move slowly outwards to the edge, taking in but trying not to think about the visual content. Now let the gaze move slowly back to the centre before closing your eyes and holding the image in your mind's eye for as long as you can before opening your eyes again and repeating the process. As you become more practised, you will find that your eye will automatically be drawn to the centre and that it rests there effortlessly on the point that symbolizes the essence of being.

Chakras

Some schools of yoga believe that there are centres of psychic energy, or chakras, placed in the sushumna, the central canal of the astral body roughly corresponding to the spinal column in the physical body. The chakras sit at various points between the base of the spine and the top of the head. Two schools of yoga, Tantric and Kundalini, practise meditation on each in turn.

Each chakra has its own yantra and its own mantra (apart from the topmost one). Starting with the lowest of them, the *muladhara,* situated between the anus and the genitals, the meditator visualizes its yantra while repeating its mantra, either inwardly or aloud, until ready to move on.

As the meditation works its way through the chakra, the latent energy of each one is released, imbuing the meditator with stronger and stronger sensations of warmth and light at the centre until, when the final meditation is completed, the physical will have merged with the spiritual—the meditator's consciousness merges with the universe.

Each chakra is adorned with its own number of lotus petals, governed by the number of the body channels that conjoin at that point in the astral body. The muladhara is adorned with four petals and its mantra is *lam.* In ascending order the chakras are the six-petalled svadhishtana and its mantra is *vam.* The manipura has ten petals and its mantra is *ram.* Next comes the anahata, with twelve petals and the mantra *yam.* Then, with sixteen petals and the mantra *ham,* is the vishuddha chakra. The ajna chakra, with its two petals and the mantra *om* is next, followed by the topmost, the sahasrara, or thousand-petal chakra, which has no mantra.

Anyone wishing to practise this form of meditation needs detailed instruction from an experienced teacher over a long period of time, but the following meditation may give you just a flavour of the full effect.

The Space between the Eyebrows Meditation

This space corresponds to the ajna chakra. Sit, kneel or lie in your usual position with your eyes closed. Gently swivel your eyeballs upwards and try to visualize them as focused on the space between your eyebrows. See how close this space is to the brain—feel its central position, visualize viewing it from the outside: now visualize it from the inside. The space between the eyebrows is a part of you. As the meditation deepens feel yourself becoming a part of that space. If unwanted thoughts intrude, mentally blow them away and return your focus to the space between the eyebrows.

It is not possible here to describe the whys and where-fores of every type of visual meditation, but the ones described below have all been used successfully by meditators the world over.

Colour Visualizing

There are many methods of using colour as a means of reaching the meditative state. The two given here are among the simplest.

For the first, sit in whichever position you favour and begin to breathe deeply. As usual, don't force the breath, but let it find its own pace and depth. When it has settled to a slow, rhythmic rate, begin to visualize the colours red, orange and yellow, flowing upwards into your solar plexus, visualizing each colour one at a time as a gently flowing river.

Spend a minute or so on each colour and then picture a stream of green flowing into the solar plexus from directly in front of you. After a minute or so, follow the green with blue, indigo and violet, each in turn flowing into you from the same source.

Once the spectrum is completed, imagine yourself bathed in a blue light before ending the meditation by opening your eyes.

Don't be put off if at first you find it difficult to visualize a colour—with practice this becomes easier.

The second method is to sit with eyes closed before focusing the thoughts on any colour you wish. Fill your mind with that colour to the exclusion of everything else and refuse to be frustrated by other thoughts that may come to mind. Wrap them slowly in colour so that they are enveloped in it. It sometimes helps to imagine an object of your chosen shade—a field of yellow corn perhaps—and gradually concentrate your thoughts on it until the field becomes totally unimportant and your mind is a canvas of yellow. (Some people who practise colour meditation begin each session by picturing an easel on which rests a blank canvas that fills up, stroke by stroke, with the chosen colour.)

Body of Light Visualizing

This is an advanced meditation. Sit comfortably with your back straight, breathing naturally. When your mind is clear and calm, visualize the space above your head as a sphere of white light slightly smaller in size than your head. Try to see it as pure and transparent, and spend several minutes concentrating on it.

See the sphere of light as representing goodness, wisdom and love—as the fulfilment of your own highest potential. Then visualize that it is getting smaller and smaller until it is about two centimetres in diameter and then slowly it begins to descend through your head towards your heart, then begins to expand once more until it spreads to every part of your body. As it does so, see it dissolve all the organs and solid parts of your body until they too become pure, formless white light.

Concentrate on the perception of your body as a mass of light and believe all your problems, negative emotions and the things that hold you back have vanished. Let any thoughts or distractions dissolve in the light, and with practice you will achieve a joyful serenity and reach a state of wholeness and perfection.

Purification Visualizing

Purification is a recurring theme in Buddhist meditation. When we see ourselves as impure or negative, that is what we become. With our self-esteem at a low ebb we feel limited and inadequate and don't give ourselves a chance to change. Believing we are pure in essence is the first step to becoming pure in practice.

This simple meditation contains the essence of purification, banishing problems and mistakes, trying to see them as temporary and not as part of our true nature.

Begin by settling comfortably into a suitable position, then concentrate on breathing normally and observing how long each inhalation and exhalation lasts. After a minute or two, imagine that all your negative energy, the mistakes you have made in the past, the things that are holding you back are leaving your body in a cloud of black smoke every time you breathe out. When you inhale, visualize that everything positive in the universe is entering your body in a stream of white light, as radiant as it is pure. Visualize it flowing to every part of your body, bathing it in its intensity.

Bubbles of Thought Meditation

Sitting in a comfortable position, visualize your mind as the smooth, calm surface of a pond. As thoughts enter your mind, see them as bubbles rising from the depths of the pond. They should be observed, not pursued, so that the conscious and deliberate following through of each thought is avoided and you become detached from it as you watch it bubble to the surface. Note the thought and then gently return to contemplating the smooth, ripple-free surface of the pond.

As time passes and you pass into deeper layers of consciousness, see yourself sinking under the surface of the pond, becoming one with it.

After about ten minutes, refocus your mind on your surroundings to bring the meditation to an end.

Inner Heat Meditation

This is an extremely advanced meditation requiring sophisticated breathing techniques as well as visualization. It is included here as an example of the most demanding meditation techniques. It was developed by a Tibetan Buddhist who believed that mental energy flows through the body within an invisible psychic nervous system made up of thousands of thin, transparent channels. The principal ones—the central, right and left channels—run parallel to and just in front of the spinal column. Pure mental energy can function within the central channel whereas diluted (deluded) energy flows through the other channels.

In our normal state, the central channel is blocked by knots of nervous energy at the various chakras discussed above. This energy blocks pure energy from the mind, making it unable to function properly.

Inner heat meditation is an excellent method for transforming powerful negative energy, helping us to develop spontaneous control over all actions of body, speech and mind.

Begin by adopting your usual meditation posture, settle your thoughts and your breathing, and visualize the central channel as a transparent, hollow tube, about the same diameter as your forefinger, running straight down the centre of the body just in front of the spinal column, from the crown of your head to the base of your spine.

Now visualize the left and right channels, slightly thinner than the central one, starting from the left and right nostrils respectively, reaching up to the top of the head then curving to run downwards on either side of the central channel before curving inwards to join the central channel about a hand's-breadth below the navel.

Take your time. There is no hurry whatsoever, and once the visualization (some people say it helps to see it as a very simple central heating system) is firmly fixed, imagine a red-hot ember the size of a seed inside the central channel level with the navel. If it helps to strengthen the visualization, see yourself reaching into a fire and taking out a small ember that you put in place.

When you really feel the intense heat, gently contract the lower pelvic muscles and see air energy rising from the lowest chakra up to the ember. Now breathe deeply through both nostrils, seeing the air travelling down the left and right channels round into the central channel, where it joins with the heat and air energy brought up from below.

When you have inhaled, swallow and push down gently with the diaphragm, compressing the energy brought down from above: the air energy is locked in, trapped from above and below.

Now hold the breath as long as possible without forcing it and concentrate on the glowing ember in the navel area, its heat now spreading through the compressed air energy.

When you breathe out, visualize the warm air rising

through the central channel, seeing it burn away the negative energies blocking each of the chakras.

Repeat the cycle seven times, intensifying the heat with each breath. By the time you breathe out for the seventh time, visualize the ember bursting into flames, shooting up the central channel and burning out the remaining negative energy in the chakras. When the flames reach the crown of the head, they melt into wonderful, almost sensual, energy that rushes down the now pure central channel, intensifying in pleasure as it passes each chakra, finally engulfing the remains of the ember and making it explode in a blissful heat that reaches every cell of your body, filling you with happiness.

If you ever succeed in this meditation, don't try to analyse the bliss, just accept it, relax, enjoy and concentrate on it calmly and in a controlled manner. It is, as said at the beginning, extremely complex, but those who have mastered it believe it is the best of all visual meditation techniques.

Visualization

Whatever we create in our lives, whether it is an omelette or a multinational corporation or a love affair, begins as an image in our minds. Inner images that we may have formed long ago, and are now outside our conscious awareness, shape and often limit our ability to make creative life choices and changes. Through image work—or visualization—it is possible to tap into, explore, and change these inner programmes that guide our lives, and to identify and bring about the future that is really right for us.

Visualization promotes relaxation and relaxation promotes visualization. Each session should start with a simple programme as follows.

Progressive Relaxation:

Clear a space

Take a moment to give yourself permission to rest. Mentally or physically clear a space, which is your personal territory and is not to be intruded on by worry, phone calls, or other internal or external demands. If there is anything you feel worried about, settle your mind by simply writing it down to look at later.

Begin to relax

Sit quietly, and focus on your breathing for a moment. Give a few long, loud sighs, feeling that each sigh starts at the top of your head and travels down through you, coming out of the soles of your feet. Whether your eyes are open or closed, roll your eyeballs up toward the ceiling, then let them drop. Notice any tension in your body and then let go of it. Imagine that you are sending a breath of peace to every part of your body. Remind yourself that you have nothing to do, and no place to go, and nothing you need worry about just now.

Relax Body and Mind

Focus on each part of your body in turn, starting with your feet. First be aware of how they feel. Now tense them, and then let them relax, sending the breath of peace there. Say to yourself, 'My foot is heavy and relaxed, and as it relaxes I feel a deep sense of peace through me.' Or simply repeat, 'Heavy and warm, warm and relaxed.' Move up your body in this way, until your whole body is included in the itinerary: 'My shoulders relaxed and peaceful, my torso and legs relaxed and peaceful, my feet warm, relaxed and peaceful....' When you reach your face and head, include your scalp, the muscles round your eyes, your lips, tongue and throat.

Let the relaxation enter your mind. Imagine that there is a little person in your head, sweeping out all the thoughts and worries. Then he paints the inside of your brain with a white light.

Allow Dark Heaviness to Descend and Lightness to Rise

If your eyes are not already closed, let them close, and imagine that your eyelids are dark, heavy blinds that are impossible to raise. Imagine that you have a dark, heavy blind at the top of your head, and pull this blind down through your body, letting the heaviness sink into the ground. Allow a feeling of lightness to emerge from the ground through your body and into your mind. Let your mind or spirit feel light, and float up, as if through a hole in the top of your head, and float out and away, like a kite in a summer sky.

Invite an Image to Deepen Relaxation

Think of a time when you were completely relaxed and feeling good about yourself. You may have been listening to music, or doing something active like swimming in the sea. When you have conjured up this picture, step into the picture, and match your breathing to that of the relaxed you in the picture.

Alternatively, in your mind travel to a place where you have been, or could be, very happy. This can be a real place or an imagined one. In this place, there is a feeling of deep peace. Creating an inner sanctuary like this can be valuable for future visualization sessions, when you can return to your own personal haven.

Countdown to Deeper Relaxation

Say to yourself, 'I am going to count down from ten to one, and with each number I will feel more and more relaxed and more in touch with my inner self.'

Create a Relaxation Cue

When you feel completely at peace, allow an image—or a word—to arise that sums up this feeling, and touch together the thumb and forefinger of either hand. Say to yourself, 'As I repeat this image or word and touch, I feel more and more relaxed and at peace, and each time I use it in the future it will bring back this wonderful feeling, and the more I use it, the better it will work.'

Now Practise your Visualization
Emerge

When you have finished your visualization session, and want to emerge from your deeply relaxed state, suggest to yourself, 'I am going to count up from one to five and with each number I will feel more and more awake, but still relaxed. When I reach five, I will open my eyes feeling relaxed and alert, as if I have woken from a long, refreshing sleep.'

The Image as Metaphor

The most basic use of visualization involves inviting an image to emerge in response to a question, and then working with the image. The images that come in this way have the powerful ability to sum up with a telling metaphor the basic structure of whatever it is you are asking about. The metaphor tends to be so accurate that the more you explore it, the more it can seem to correspond on every level and in every detail, not only with the specific problem but with your life as a whole. Suddenly the implicit becomes explicit and a resolution emerges.

Begin by encouraging an image to emerge, and then study it from a number of perspectives. Then enter the image, and deepen the exploration from inside it. Finally, look back and get a sense of what led up to the present situation, and look forward to what is the next step for you. Try out this step in your mind.

Begin by clearing a space and relaxing, as described above. Now invite an image to emerge. Say: 'I would like to allow an image to emerge of an animal, plant or object that somehow represents who I am or what I need to know at this moment in my life: the first image that comes to mind, whether as a word, a picture, a sound or a fleeting sense. This image is now sitting in the chair opposite.'

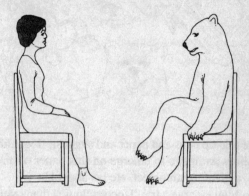

When the image emerges, say, 'Thank you, Unconscious. I appreciate the gift.'

If nothing happens, try the following strategies until something emerges:

- Looking back over the past few days, remembering everything I have seen, I notice one memory image that seems to draw my attention. That image is now in the chair opposite me.
- I imagine that my unconscious is like a wonderful rich sea full of treasures, and floating up out of this sea is an image that represents who I am or what I need to know at this moment in my life. This image is now sitting opposite me.

- Take felt-tip pens and paper and suggest, 'I would like
  to allow an image to emerge on this paper of an animal, a plant, or an object, etc [as above].'

  If nothing emerges, try, 'Unconscious, I thank you for
  your efforts to protect me, but I would like to explore
  these images. Please help me to do so in a safe and natural way…'

  As a last resort, take the 'nothingness' or the blank-
  ness of not having an image to be your image, and explore that.

Study the Image

Allow the image to become clearer. What does it look
like? What colour is it? Does it make a sound? Does it
have a smell? Does it move, and if so, how? What is its
relationship to the environment?

Imagine that your mind or spirit is free to study it

from every perspective—from above, underneath and every side. What more do you notice?

Become the Image

Step into the image. Get up and sit in the chair where you saw the image, or just step into the image in your mind. Feel it absolutely, for example, the wind blowing through your wings if you are a bird, or the earth around your roots if you are a plant. Now return to your own seat and question the image. Change seats when you are the image, answering the questions. As you tune into the image, questions relevant to your own situation will arise, but here are some suggestions:

- Tell me about yourself.
- What is the essence of being you—the boatness of the boat, the bearness of the bear, or whatever the image is.

- Where are you? What can you see and feel around you?
- How does it feel to be you?
- What is the best thing about your life and what is the worst thing?
- What do you hope for and what do you fear?
- Do you feel at home in the world around you or at conflict with it?
- Is there a problem that needs solving?
- What else do you notice about being you at this moment in your life?

Get a Sense of the History

Ask the image about the background of the present situation:

- What led up to your present situation?
- Was there a time when things were different?
- When? How were they different? How and when did the change take place?

Get a Sense of the Possibilities

Ask:

- What's next? What do you need to do to make your life better or to feel more complete?
- What seems right? What should happen?
- If you could wave a magic wand over your life, how would you like it to be?

It is now x time later (x can be ten minutes, a day, a year, or whatever period you like) and you feel good about your life. What is happening now. What did you do?

If an answer emerges, imagine it and enjoy it. If you get stuck without an answer at this stage, ask:

- What's stopping you from moving forward?
- What do you fear will happen?
- What feels useful about the seemingly negative aspects of the way you are now?

Let your mind float up from your body and look down, studying the image from above. If you could tell it something from this perspective that would help it, what would it be?

As soon as an answer emerges to these questions, follow through by suggestion, 'do it, and enjoy it,' and continue to ask, 'What happens next?' until you reach a natural resting point.

Appreciate and Emerge

Tune back into the original image. What is happening now? Is there a change? How do you feel about the future? Review the pictures and feelings you have just been through, and notice the best picture/feeling in all that. Allow yourself to feel/be that again, and notice exactly what it is like, both physically and emotionally, so that you can recognize that state of mind and body in future.

Reflect

Using your conscious resources, spend a few moments reflecting on what you have just been through, and also keep the image in the back of your mind over the next few days and continue this process. Ask yourself:

'How does this image reflect my life as it is and has been? What do I feel good about as I look at this clarification of my underlying programme? What do I feel uneasy about? How does the image fit in with previous images I have had of myself?'

Look Forward

Ask yourself:

'What are the practical implications of all this? What does it really mean to make this change? What do I need to do to take the next step?'

'If I had already made this change, suggested by the image, how would I deal differently with this problem and with life in general? What would a day in my life be like if I had this new image in the background? How does it differ from a typical day now? What could stop me from making this change? How do I usually sabotage myself?'

Emerge

When you are ready to emerge from this deeply relaxed state, suggest the following: 'I'm going to count up from one to five and when I say five, I will open my eyes, feeling relaxed and alert, feeling better than before, as if I've had a long refreshing sleep, and bringing back with me the best feelings, pictures, and insights from my explorations. One, two—coming up to the surface, eyelids lightening; three—alert but still relaxed; four, five—eyes open.'

At various moments during the next few days or weeks, ask yourself how you might experience things differently if you were the image-being at its best. Or ask it for advice: 'What do you think I should do now?'

Every now and then, tune in to the image-being to see what state it is in. Is the bear feeling friendly, or is it running around in a confused way, or is it hiding in fright? This is a good indication of your present state of mind.

My Future Self

This exercise can be used for any time period in the future. It is useful to start by imagining your eighty-year-old self, so as to get a sense of your long-term goals. Then choose whatever shorter time period feels most relevant to you.

Clear a Space and Relax, as above. Suggest to yourself: 'I am on a spaceship zooming off the face of the earth. I return to earth at age eighty (or six months/five years/ten years later—whatever period you want to work with) and I discover my future self—completely happy with my life.'

Explore the image of your future self, in the given period of the future. Make the image as vivid and concrete as possible: what are you wearing? How do you feel in your body, mind and spirit? Ask yourself: 'What is the good feeling I have? What was the most important thing I did or experienced to reach this good feeling? Looking back at the younger me, what do I notice? What do I want to whisper that would make life easier for him or her?'

Having established a clear image, ask it specific questions:

- How have my relationships—with friends, family and colleagues been?
- What did I accomplish or create and how exactly did I go about it?
- How was my self-esteem and how did I take care of myself physically?
- How do I feel about the way life has treated me? What did I learn about life itself?
- What do I feel best about? What could I tell the younger me that would help him or her?

This exercise can also be done from the negative point of view:

It's x time from now and I feel absolutely terrible.

What is this terrible feeling? What is the most important thing I did to make it happen? Reviewing my personal and professional life, where did I go wrong? What could I tell the younger me that will help him or her not to end up like this? Finally, before and after emerging, reflect on what all this means and what the implications are. Decide on specific and practical ways in which you can use these new insights to improve your life now.

Quick Visualization

This is a very useful technique when you want to re-lax—before an interview, a party, or any stressful situation.

Simply say to yourself: 'It's the end of this event and I feel really good about it. What is this good feeling? What did I do to bring it about?'

Or: 'It's the end of this event and I feel really bad about it. What is this awful feeling? What did I do to bring it about? With this hindsight, what steps can I take to avoid it?'

If you have decided on a life change or goal that you want to achieve, a useful exercise is:

The Cinema Exercise

Clear a space and relax, as above.

Now imagine that you are in your own private cinema. You are sitting in the middle of the cinema, with the screen in front of you.

Allow a picture to emerge on the screen as you are now, before you have achieved the goal. Examine the picture. How do you feel about the person? Allow yourself to accept and support him or her, even if you do not completely approve of his or her behaviour. Recognize they are doing their best at the moment, until they are able, with your help, to move on. Now let the picture move off the screen, to the left, into the past. This is how you were, but no longer are.

Now allow a picture of yourself to emerge as you will be, after you have achieved your goal or made this life change. Look at this new picture. How is it different from the old picture? In your imagination, leave your seat, walk up to the screen and step into the picture. How does it feel to be this person? How is it different from the other person you were? Become clear how you act and what it is that makes this form of action so successful. Spend a day as this person, noticing all the details of your life, from how you get up, through the day of work and leisure, to going to bed.

Still living as the new person, imagine that you have two helpers, who may be real or imaginary people. One is a supporter, who cheers you on, and one is an expert at what you are doing who can advise you. Who are they? Ask them whatever you like and see what they say. Step into their image, to experience the feeling of operating expertly, and of loving and supporting the new person you have become.

Look back and see what led up to this point. Look at the person you were before. What steps did you take to become this new person?

Now step out of the screen and go back to your seat. Look at the person on the screen and realize that this is really as you could be and will be. Make a decision that this goal is possible, desirable and one to which you have a right. Decide that you will put all your energy and intentions into becoming that person.

Put the image on the screen into a bubble and say to yourself, 'I fully intend for this to happen, and I release it.' Send the balloon off, out of sight.

Before and after emerging, reflect on the concrete implications of what you have learned, and look forward to see what you intend to do in a practical sense to make your vision come true. Spend some time every day practising being the person you will be after having made the life change.

When you want to do something that has been weighing on your mind, and about which you have been procrastinating, allow an image of yourself doing it to emerge on the screen, put the image in a bubble, and intend and release. This cuts down anxiety and gets the

problem out of your mind and into the area of potentials
waiting to be actualized.

Aromatherapy

In the past our sense of smell was crucial to our survival—we could smell intruders, sense which plants were poisonous and track game through their odour. Obviously our reliance on this sense has lessened, but we are still extremely susceptible to smell—both personal and environmental. We all have our own unique smell (pheromones), apart from body odour, and while our recognition may be subconscious, it has more effect on our responses and behaviour than we may realize.

Most of us find comfort and relaxation through our sense of smell every day. Gardeners often choose flowers and plants because of their smell; we add attractive scents to our toiletries and frequently choose our remedies for colds and sore throats because of their aroma. Few cooks eschew the use of aromatic herbs, and it can be no coincidence that herbs chosen for their flavour and fragrance, such as ginger, rosemary and thyme, also stimulate our gastric juices. Similarly, aromatherapy uses essential oils extracted from aromatic plants and trees to comfort and relax as well as to stimulate the human body.

A holistic medicine, aromatherapy shares the same

principles as acupuncture, reflexology and herbal medicine. These arts are complementary and work on the principle of promoting mental serenity and bodily health by treating our person as one entity. Essential oils can affect mood, alleviate fatigue, reduce anxiety and promote relaxation. When inhaled they work on the brain and nervous system through stimulation of the olfactory nerves. When absorbed through the skin, stronger components are released into the bloodstream.

The ancient Egyptians were probably the first to become aware of the value of essential oils and even imported them from other countries. Hieroglyphics show how their high priests employed them in sophisticated medicinal and cosmetic preparations.

The art eventually reached Britain through trade with the Greeks and the Romans, with the earliest written British record appearing in the 13th century. Interest waned in the 19th century due to the development of the chemical copies of plant oils. But the 20th century's renewed interest in natural treatments and therapies has pushed oil extraction and implementation techniques to the forefront of the holistic industry. Pure essential oils are now used in toiletries, foods and medicines, and their properties are scientifically recognized.

The raw materials of aromatherapy, the essential oils, are derived from plants, fruits and herbs. Their chemistry is complex, but usually includes alcohols, esters, ketones, aldehydes and terpenes. These oils are present in tiny droplets in roots, flowers, barks, rinds and resins—all in varying quantities. They are very kinetic by nature and are constantly changing in chemical composition, from day to day and season to season. Soil and weather also have a huge effect on their make-up, so they have to be picked with scientific precision. Often they are very expensive due to complicated extraction procedures and the requirements of large quantities of the raw material. For instance, it takes 2000 kilograms of jasmine to produce one kilogram of essential oil.

There are many methods employed in extracting the oils, such as hand expression, enfleurage and maceration, but the most modern and most commonly used method is steam distillation. Making use of the volatile nature of the oils and the fact that they are insoluble in water, this method also impregnates the steam with the fragrant essence of the water, thus creating useful by-products. Orange and rose water are two popular examples. Because of their fragile nature, oils must be kept in their bottles in a cool dark place to protect their properties.

Essential oils are very adaptable. They can be added to a bath, either individually or blended, where the steam releases their perfume. Add a total of 5–8 drops to a full bath just before getting in and gently agitate the water to disperse the oil. While you relax in the bath, a small amount of oil is absorbed by the skin and the rest is slowly evaporated by the heat of the water to make you feel more uplifted and relaxed. An aromatic bath is one of the easiest and most enjoyable forms of relaxation therapy. The oils can also be inhaled directly from a bottle or they can be incorporated into massage oil. Pure essential oils should not be used on the skin unless diluted in a vegetable or lotion base. For application, add a maximum of one drop to each millilitre of base oil or lotion. You can use one or more essential oils, but the total amount added should not exceed the quantities given above. Massage is of particular benefit as human beings derive enormous comfort from the touch of others. The action of rubbing a sore joint or painful sprain is instinctive to everyone, which is why the use of essential oils, combined with massage, is so effective in relieving pain and tension.

When rubbed into the skin, essential oils will permeate the pores and hair follicles and work their way around the body. Each oil is credited with its own specific therapeutic qualities, while all have antibiotic, antiseptic and anti-inflammatory properties to a greater or lesser degree. Used correctly, they are capable of boosting the immune system, stimulating cell growth, improving circulation and relieving fluid retention. They are at their best, however, in relieving the stresses that undermine our immune systems.

Essential oils can also be used in vaporizers to create an uplifting or relaxing mood. Simple pottery vaporizers are available, in which oils are heated in water above a candle. Or you can buy a sophisticated electrical gadget that vaporizes the oils. It is great fun to create your own blends, which permeate a room or a house and help you to unwind after a hard day at work, or even set the mood for a party—orange and pine at Christmas, for example.

Aromatherapy oils are a very useful tool in the fight against stress. A therapeutic massage using these oils is one of the most pleasant ways of relieving stress and finding a wonderful, liberating sense of relaxation.

Oils for Relaxation

Basil
Basil helps to invigorate the body and spirit, refreshes the mind to improve concentration, and is especially effective when tired. It is an excellent nerve tonic after a stressful day. It has a sweet, liquorice-like fragrance, and blends well with lavender, bergamot, clary sage and geranium.

Benzoin Tincture
A warm, soothing, comforting oil. Add to carrier oil or cream to protect skin against chapping or cracking.

Bergamot

The lovely light citrus aroma of this oil relaxes and re-freshes. Can be used in a vaporizer to disperse unpleasant smells. Add one drop to cooled boiled water as a mouthwash. It also blends well with other oils.

Warning: Do not use this oil on the skin before going out into strong sunlight or using a sunbed: it can increase susceptibility to sunburn.

Black Pepper

One of the oldest known spices, the oil's pungent aroma has a stimulating and warming effect. It blends well with rosemary, marjoram and lavender, but should be used in small amounts.

Warning: Black pepper can be a skin irritant, so must be used with care.

Cajeput

Improves mood and increases resistance to infections. A very good oil for unwinding, it can also be used in a steam inhalation to help clear the nasal passages, and is also useful in treating oily skin and spots.

Warning: Cajeput is a stimulant and an irritant and must be used with care.

Camomile, Roman

This oil is known for its strong, soothing effect on the

mind and body. It can be used to calm nerves, soothe headaches and alleviate menstrual disorders. Ever since Peter Rabbit was put to bed with a cup of camomile tea, after his lucky escape from the gardener, camomile has been popular as an effective aid to peaceful sleep. It is also one of the few essential oils that can be used on inflamed skin conditions.

Camphor

This oil can be used to help alleviate cold symptoms that make it hard to relax. It is also useful for treating oily or spotty skin.

Warning: Camphor should be used sparingly and completely avoided by those suffering from epilepsy.

Cardamom Seed

The sweet, spicy, warming fragrance of cardamom has been enjoyed since the days of the ancient Egyptians, who used it as a perfume and incense. It can be used as an aid to digestion and makes a refreshing, relaxing bath oil.

Cedarwood

Recognized as a therapeutic oil from ancient times, cedarwood has a soothing and steadying effect. The oil is also useful for protecting oily and blemished skin, and as an inhalant it helps to relieve coughs and colds.

Warning: Do not use cedarwood during pregnancy.

Cinnamon

A warming and stimulating oil that is traditionally used to alleviate digestive disorders. It also has antiseptic properties and has a cleansing effect.

Warning: Cinnamon is a powerful irritant and must not be used directly on the skin.

Clary Sage

Noted for its soothing, relaxing and warming effect, it contains a hormone-like compound similar to oestrogen and is wonderful for regulating hormonal balance—especially premenstrually and at the menopause. Massaging the abdomen will bring relaxation through relief of menstrual discomfort.

Warning: Do not use during pregnancy.

Clove

An antiseptic oil used to relieve toothache—what Robert Burns called 'the Hell o' 'a diseases' and about the most unrelaxing state there is to be in.

Warning: Clove is a powerful skin irritant and should be used carefully. Do not use during pregnancy.

Coriander

A sweet-smelling, spicy essence, it makes a good massage blend to relieve stiffness and muscle ache. It is refreshing and stimulating in the bath.

Cypress
With its smoky, woody fragrance, it refreshes, restores and tones. It is an astringent oil useful for refreshing and caring for oily and blemished skin. As a natural deodorant, it can also be used as an antiperspirant and is good for sweaty feet. Blends well with lavender and sandalwood.

Eucalyptus
This is a powerful antiseptic used to alleviate the symptoms of colds and flu. Use as a chest rub and in a vaporizer to keep the air germ-free. Blends well with lavender and pine.

Fennel
Fennel has a sweet, aniseed-like aroma, which makes it pleasant for skin care. As a massage oil it is good for the digestive system, and can promote breast firming and milk production, but use sparingly.
Warning: Fennel can be a skin irritant. Do not use it on young children. Do not use if pregnant. Do not use if suffering from epilepsy.

Frankincense

This oil soothes, warms and aids meditation. It has been used for centuries and burnt on altars and in temples. It has a comforting effect, and by slowing down breathing and controlling tension it helps to focus the mind. It is excellent for toning and caring for mature or ageing skin: it is supposed to have rejuvenating qualities and, for this reason, the Egyptians used it in face masks.

Geranium

One of the most relaxing oils, geranium balances the mind and body. It soothes, restores and maintains stability of the emotions. It is also useful in massage for treating eczema and proriasis. It blends well with other floral oils and, mixed with lavender and bergamot, produces a delightful room freshener.

Ginger

A warm and penetrating oil that is good for nausea and sickness. Blend with orange for warming winter baths. It blends especially well with orange and other citrus oils. Use in small amounts.

Grapefruit

This essence refreshes and uplifts the spirit. It has a lovely fresh aroma that can help with nervous exhaustion.

Warning: Do not use grapefruit on the skin in direct sunlight.

Hyssop

This fragrance was sacred to the Greeks and the Hebrews, who used hyssop brooms to clean out sacred places. It has a warm and vibrant aroma that can be used to promote alertness and clarity of thought. When used as a fragrancer it can help to protect rooms from infection. It is also used for treating colds and flu.

Warning: This powerful oil should not be used when pregnant, or if suffering from epilepsy or high blood pressure.

Jasmine

This oil is emotionally warming. It also relaxes, soothes, uplifts and enhances self-confidence. It is good for stress and general anxiety. It only needs to be used in very small quantities. It is very expensive because large numbers of blossoms must be gathered at night, when their scent is at its highest, to produce only a few drops of oil.

Juniper

Its fresh woody aroma tones and stimulates. It has a cleansing effect on the body and a calming effect on the emotions and is reputed to strengthen the immune system.

Warning: Juniper should not be used when pregnant.

Lavender

This is undoubtedly the most versatile and useful oil, and no home should be without it. It relaxes, soothes, restores and balances your body and mind. Excellent for refreshing tired muscles, feet and head. Wonderful for a relaxing bath before bed—and if you add a few drops to the water in your steam iron when ironing your sheets, you will drift off to sleep as if in a field of lavender flowers. A drop can also be added to the pillow. Blends happily with most other oils.

Lemon

An astringent and antiseptic oil that cleanses, refreshes, cools and stimulates. Useful for oily skins, it can be used to lighten dull, stained hands or to tone and condition nails and cuticles. It blends well with other oils.
Warning: Do not use lemon on the skin in direct sunlight. Dilute to 1 per cent and use only three drops in the bath as it may cause skin irritation.

Lemongrass

An antiseptic and astringent oil that has a refreshing, cleansing and stimulating effect on the mind and body. Its sweet, powerful, lemony aroma makes it a good choice as a refreshing and deodorizing room fragrance.

Warning: Dilute to 1 per cent and use only three drops in a bath as it may cause skin irritation.

Marjoram

Popular with the ancient Greeks, it soothes, comforts and warms. Useful on tired muscles and for massage, it can also be used to regulate the nervous system and treat insomnia. It is pleasant in a hot bath, especially blended with lavender.

Warning: Do not use during pregnancy. It has a sedative effect, so always use carefully.

Melissa

A popular garden herb known as 'lemon balm', this has a soothing, but uplifting, effect on the mind and body.

Warning: Do not use melissa on the skin in direct sunlight. Dilute to 1 per cent and use only three drops in a bath as it may cause skin irritation.

Myrrh

This is a smoky, mysterious oil. Add to a cream for protecting skin against cracking and chapping in the cold. Add to gargle and mouthwash.

Warning: Do not use myrrh during pregnancy.

Neroli

This is the most effective oil for relieving the symptoms

of stress. Its exquisite aroma soothes, relaxes, uplifts the spirit and helps enhance self-confidence. It can be used to improve sluggish circulation, and to relieve tension and anxiety.

Orange
A warm, comforting oil that soothes, restores and uplifts the spirit. Blend with spicy oils for cheering baths. Use as a massage oil for the digestive system. It also encourages restful sleep.
Warning: Do not use on the skin in direct sunlight. Dilute to 2 per cent and use only four or five drops in a bath as it may cause irritation.

Patchouli
A sweet, musky oil that soothes and uplifts the spirit. Useful in protecting dry, mature or blemished skin.

Palma Rosa
This is distilled from a grass that grows in Brazil and Central America. It is very useful for treating skin infections and as a tonic.

Peppermint
One of the most important essential oils, it stimulates, refreshes, cools, restores and uplifts the mind and body. Add to a massage blend for the digestive system. It is

excellent for refreshing tired head and feet. Sniff from the bottle or from a drop on a handkerchief to revive energy during long journeys. Add a few drops to the car dashboard to help stay alert, stimulate clear thinking and remain fresh. Blended with rosemary and juniper, it makes an excellent morning bath.

Warning: Some aromatherapists warn against the use of peppermint when pregnant. Dilute to 1 per cent and use no more than 3 drops in the bath as it may cause irritation to sensitive skin.

Pine

Pine has a strong, fresh, resinous aroma and a powerful antiseptic and invigorating quality.

Warning: Dilute and use with care as pine oil may cause skin irritation.

Rose Otto

Called the 'queen of flowers', it has an exquisite aroma that is emotionally soothing and helps to maintain self-confidence. It is excellent for skin care: perfect for dry, mature, ageing or thread-veined skin.

Warning: Avoid during the first four months of pregnancy.

Rosemary

A popular oil that has a variety of mental and physical

benefits. It refreshes tired muscles, clears the mind and aids concentration. It combats fatigue and clears a stuffy atmosphere.

Warning: Do not use rosemary if pregnant, have high blood pressure or suffer from epilepsy.

Rosewood

This oil has a pleasant and flowery aroma that is relaxing and deodorizing. Add to massage oil to help combat tired muscles—especially after vigorous exercise. It has a steadying and balancing effect on nerves, and is useful during exams. It is also a good antidepressant and may help to alleviate migraine.

Sage

This oil has a calming effect on the central nervous system. It may also help with menstrual and digestive disorders.

Warning: Do not use sage when pregnant or suffering from epilepsy.

Sandalwood

This oil has a rich, woody, sweet aroma, and is traditionally burnt as an aid to meditation.

Tea Tree

This oil has powerful antiseptic, antifungal and antiviral

properties. It acts as a stimulant to the immune system and has a wide range of medicinal uses.

Warning: May cause irritation to sensitive skins.

Thyme

This has been used for centuries as a medicinal and culinary herb. It has a strong pungent aroma and can be used as a vapour to alleviate nasal congestion.

Warning: Do not use when pregnant or if you have high blood pressure. Dilute to no more than 2 per cent before use. It may cause irritation to sensitive skins.

Ylang Ylang

The name means 'flower of flowers'. This sweet oil has a soothing and relaxing effect in times of tension and stress. It is also ideal for both oily and dry skins and can be used as a hair rinse: use two drops in water. It blends well with lemon and bergamot.

Suggested Blends of Oils for Relaxation and Relief from Stress

For general relaxation:

Bergamot: 9 drops; Geranium: 11 drops; Ginger: 10 drops. Grapefruit: 15 drops; Rosemary: 11 drops; Palma Rosa: 5 drops; Neroli: 7 drops; Lavender; 3 drops; Lemon: 20 drops.

For anxiety:

Lavender: 10 drops; Geranium: 10 drops; Palma Rosa: 10 drops.

For depression and insomnia:

Clary Sage: 15 drops; Lemon: 10 drops; Lavender: 5 drops.

For exhaustion:

Lemon: 10 drops; Clary sage: 5 drops; Lavender: 15 drops.

Suggestions for use

As a massage oil: Add your chosen single oil or blend to a base oil, which can be almond, hazelnut, peach kernel, apricot kernel, grapeseed, soya, peanut etc. Add a maximum of 1 drop to each millilitre of base vegetable oil. Add the aromatherapy oils to the base oil (ask your chemist for a brown glass bottle with its volume stamped on the glass on the bottom to make this easier). Turn the bottle upside down a few times, and then roll it briskly between your palms to disperse the oil. A teaspoon of oil is enough for most body massages.

In the bath: Run the bath, then add the essential oil or oils—up to a maximum of 8 drops. A small glassful of milk can be thrown on to the surface of the water and the oil dropped on to this and dispersed lightly with the hand to help the oils spread evenly. Close the bathroom door to shut in the vapours, and soak for at least ten minutes, relaxing and breathing deeply. For the ultimate relaxation experience, burn a candle at the bath side (make sure it is in a secure container—especially if your bath is made of plastic). Sip a cup of camomile tea when soaking in a bath with soothing oils. Before an evening out, add uplifting oils to the bath and sip a glass of champagne.

As an inhalation: Pour hot (not boiling) water into a bowl and add 2–3 drops of essential oil. Cover your head with a towel and lean over the bowl with your face about 25 cm (10 inches) away and your eyes closed. Breathe deeply through your nose for about a minute.

In the sauna: Use 2 drops per 600 ml (1 pint) of water. Mix into the water and throw on to the heat source as usual. Use only eucalyptus, tea tree or pine oils because they enter the body with inhalation and exit by perspiration. They are excellent cleansers and detoxifiers, and so add to the revitalizing effects of the sauna.

In the shower: After having washed as usual, add the essential oil to your sponge or flannel and rub this over yourself briskly while still standing under the running hot water. Breathe in the steam deeply as you rub.

On candles: Light the candle, wait until the wax begins to melt and then add 1–2 drops of essential oil. Be careful not to get the oils on to the wick, because these oils are inflammable.

In diffusers: Use 1–6 drops in the diffuser—which can be electric or heated by a candle. The oils are heated by this method, allowing their molecules to be released into the air.

On a light bulb: Add 1–2 drops of essential oil to the bulb of a table lamp when it is not switched on and is quite cool. The heat of the bulb when it is switched on will disperse the oils through the room. Aromatherapy rings can also be bought that fit on to light bulbs.

By a radiator: Put 1–9 drops of essential oil on to a cotton wool ball and wedge it beside the radiator pipe where it is in contact with the heat.

As a room spray: Use 4–6 drops per 300 ml (½ pint) water in a new plant sprayer. Add the oil to warm water and shake well before use. Spray in rooms, avoiding wooden surfaces.

In the fire: Add a drop of cypress, pine, cedar or sandalwood oil to a log and leave for half an hour before using. One log on a fire should give off enough relaxing, forest smells.

Autogenics

This is another relaxation technique derived from the principles of Eastern meditation. The participant learns to switch off the fight or flight response to stressful situations through progressive self-relaxation.

The system was originally devised by Johannes H. Schultz, a German psychiatrist and hypnotherapist. The technique is a combination of controlled breathing, hypnotherapy and positive thinking. Autogenics places heavy emphasis on self-belief and self-determination. Many studies of the system have confirmed that it is an excellent technique of deep relaxation, and can help to alleviate or control many stress-related disorders, such as phobias, anxiety, high blood pressure, migraines, insomnia and muscle tension. It also helps to improve concentration and overall coordination.

Many trained autogenics practitioners are also qualified psychotherapists or counsellors. They help to educate a person to control and reduce stress responses, to achieve deep relaxation, promote inner harmony, and restore emotional and physical wellbeing.

Biofeedback

This refers to the use of monitoring equipment to measure and control levels of relaxation. Training can be given after the scientific data is examined.

Although great feats of body and mind control have been reported in Eastern medicine for centuries, it has only been in the past two decades that Western medicine has accepted the fact that humans can, indeed, regulate their own heart rate, circulation, temperature, muscle tension, and other body functions that were mostly thought to operate only automatically. That acceptance came largely through the development of the biofeedback machine, which teaches people to become aware of various body functions and to control them with conscious intent, using relaxation and mental imagery techniques.

Today biofeedback is widely used for the treatment of chronic pain and stress-related disorders. Even astronauts have used biofeedback to control the nausea of space sickness.

If you go for biofeedback therapy, you will be asked to sit in a comfortable chair in front of a machine that looks like a TV set. Electrode sensors (wires) from the biofeedback machine will be taped to your body, usually on your forehead, neck, back or forefinger. With the help of relaxing music or a taped voice that suggests relaxation techniques, you will be asked to reduce the muscle tension throughout your body. Later you may also be asked to slow your heart rate, even to warm your hands by increasing their blood flow. While you're trying to accomplish these feats, the machine measures your muscle tension, heart rate and blood flow, and 'feeds back' how well you are doing. This feedback can be in the form of audible beeps, pictures, or graphic lines.

After learning what the correct response feels like by working with the machine and practising at home, you should eventually be able to achieve the same response without the machine.

Herbalism

The use of medicinal herbs to alleviate illness and promote feelings of relaxation is based on ancient techniques. When used properly, traditional herbs are non-addictive, have no side effects and can have impressive results. Herbs are particularly useful in treating nervous tension, depression, insomnia, PMS (premenstrual syndrome), nervous headaches and migraines. Herbal medicines are also extremely important in helping to reduce stress by their effects on the immune, circulatory and neuromuscular systems.

Herbalism is sometimes maligned as a collection of home-made remedies to be applied in a placebo fashion to one symptom or another, provided the ailment is not too serious and provided there is a powerful chemical wonder drug at the ready to suppress any 'real' symptoms. We often forget, however, that botanical medicine provides a complete system of healing and disease prevention. It is the oldest and most natural form of medicine. Its record of efficacy and safety spans centuries and covers every country worldwide. Because herbal medicine is holistic medicine, it is, in fact, able to look beyond the symptoms to the underlying systemic imbalance; when skilfully applied by a trained practitioner, herbal medicine offers very real and permanent solutions to concrete problems, many of them seemingly intractable to pharmaceutical intervention.

Nowhere is the efficacy of herbalism more evident than in problems related to the nervous system. Stress, anxiety, tension and depression are intimately connected with most illness, Few health practitioners would argue about the role of nervous anxiety in pathology. Nervous tension is generally acknowledged by doctors to contribute to duodenal and gastric ulceration, ulcerative colitis, irritable bowel syndrome and many other gut-related pathologies.

We know also, from physiology, that when a person is depressed, the secretion of hydrochloric acid—one of the main digestive juices—is also reduced so that digestion and absorption are rendered less efficient. Anxiety, on the other hand, can lead to the release of adrenaline and stimulate the over-production of hydrochloric acid and result in a state of acidity that may exacerbate the pain of an inflamed ulcer. In fact, whenever the voluntary nervous system (our conscious anxiety) interferes with the autonomic processes (the automatic nervous regulation that in health is never made conscious), illness is the result.

Herbalists rely on their knowledge of botanical remedies to rectify this type of human malfunction. The medicinal herbalist will treat a stubborn dermatological problem using alternative herbal medicines specific to the skin problem, and then apply circulatory stimulants to aid in the removal of toxins from the area, with remedies to reinforce other organs of elimination, such as the liver and kidneys. Under such natural treatment, free of any discomfiting side effects, the patient can feel confident and relaxed—perhaps for the first time in many months.

Curiously, this is an approach that has never been taken up by orthodox medicine. There, the usual treatment of skin problems involves suppression of symptoms with steroids. However, the use of conventional antihistamines or benzodiazepines often achieves less lasting benefit to the patient because of the additional burden of side effects, such as drowsiness, increased toxicity, and long-term drug dependence.

Herbs, on the other hand, are free from toxicity and habituation. Because they are organic substances and not manmade synthetic molecules, they possess an affinity for the human organism. They are extremely efficient in balancing the nervous system—restoring a sense of wellbeing and relaxation is necessary for optimum health and for the process of self-healing.

Naturally, the choice of a treatment should be based upon a thorough health assessment and the experience and training of a qualified herbal practitioner. The herbalist will then prepare and prescribe herbal remedies in a variety of different forms, such as infusions, loose teas, suppositories, inhalants, lotions, tinctures, tablets and pills. Many of these preparations are available for home use from chemists, health shops and mail-order suppliers.

Herbs for Relaxation

Camomile

This has a relaxing effect on the mind and body. It is an excellent sedative for anxiety and muscle tenseness. Many people enjoy its benefits in the form of camomile tea.

Valerian

This is the ideal tranquillizer. The rhizomes of the plant contain a volatile oil (which includes valerianic acid), volatile alkaloids (including chatinine), and iridoids (valepotriates), which have been shown to reduce anxiety and depression. So effective is valerian in relieving anxiety while maintaining normal mental awareness, that it enables us to continue the most complicated mental exercise without drowsiness, loss of consciousness or depression. For all these reasons, valerian has been usefully taken before an examination or a driving test.

Peppermint

This is effective for treating digestive discomfort, perhaps brought on by a lack of relaxation when eating. It relieves indigestion, flatulence, constipation and nausea. Peppermint is also a good mind tonic, helping to clarify ideas and focus concentration. It is also helpful in alleviating the symptoms of colds and flu. Peppermint and camomile tea is thought to be effective in reducing the pain of tension headaches and migraines.

Vervain

This is not only effective against depression but also strongly supports the detoxifying function of the liver. Its French name is still 'Herbe Sacre'; an old English name is 'Holy Wort'—it was one of the seven sacred herbs of the Druids. Today we know that the antispasmodic qualities of vervain are largely due to the glycoside verbenalin. Recent Chinese research has linked the plant with dilation of the arteries in the brain: a likely explanation of its usefulness in treating migraine, especially when the problem is accompanied by liver congestion. It is certainly of use in treating exhaustion and depression, and so promoting relaxation.

St John's Wort

Also called *Hypericum perforatum*, St John's Wort has analgesic and anti-inflammatory properties, with important local applications to neuralgia and sciatica. Systemically, its sedative properties are based on the glycoside hypericin (a red pigment), which makes it applicable to neurosis and irritability. Many herbalists use it extensively as a background remedy.

Lemon Balm
This herb is both carminative and antispasmodic, and is active specifically on that part of the vagus nerve that may interfere with the harmonious functioning of the heart and the stomach. Recent research has indicated that the action of the volatile oil begins within the limbic system of the brain and subsequently operates directly upon the vagus nerve and all the organs that are innervated by it. Accordingly, neurasthenia (complete nervous prostration), migraine and nervous gastropathy are all amenable to its healing powers.

Lime Flowers
These are thought to be helpful in controlling anxiety and hyperactivity. They are also effective for treating insomnia, high blood pressure and for soothing muscles and nerves.

Borage
This is an effective mind tonic that helps to alleviate headaches, migraine and depression.

Oats

Oats are some of the greatest herbal restoratives of the nervous system. The plant contains a nervine alkaloid that is helpful in angina and in cardiac insufficiency. It has also been used in the treatment of addiction to narcotics, tobacco and alcohol.

Soothing herbal drinks

Warm Milk and Honey

Perhaps with a dash of cinnamon, this is an ideal drink to take at bedtime. It will help you relax and ward off insomnia.

Hop Tea

Three hop cones, or heads, infused in a cup of boiling water whenever you begin to feel excessively tense, is a marvellous remedy for anxiety and insomnia.

A Soothing Herb Tea to Sustain a Feeling of Equilibrium

25g (1 oz) each dried camomile flowers, lime flowers, hibiscus blossoms and marigold flowers

15g ($^{1}/_{2}$ oz) each dried peppermint leaves and vervain

1 teaspoon whole fenugreek seeds

100g (4 oz) Lapsang Souchong tea

Mix all the ingredients together and store in a dark air-tight container. Use 1 teaspoon to 300 ml ($^1/_2$ pint) of boiling water in a tea pot and leave to infuse for five minutes before straining and serving with a slice of lemon and a teaspoon of honey if desired. This is a very calming tea that soothes feelings of anxiety. It also helps to clear your head and settle an upset tummy. One cup taken morning and night will promote a feeling of well-being.

Another Calming Tea, Especially Good for the Nerves

1 teaspoon each grated valerian root and dried mint
$^1/_2$ teaspoon each dried camomile and lavender flowers
600 ml (1 pint) boiling water

Infuse the dry ingredients in the water for 15 minutes then strain and take a glass three times a day for one week only.

Two Tonic Teas to Sip when Feeling Depressed

Sip either 2 teaspoons of dandelion and 1 of basil infused in 600 ml (1 pint) of boiling water, or 2 teaspoons each of nettle, basil and melissa infused in 600 ml (1 pint) of boiling water.

A Tonic Tea to Relieve Stress and Anxiety

1 tablespoon each fresh dandelion and nettle tops
1 teaspoon each fresh blackcurrant and borage leaves
600 ml (1 pint) boiling water

Steep the greenery in the water for five minutes. Strain and drink with lemon and honey.

Dock Wine

Dock is one of the great tonic herbs because it is extremely high in iron. Here is a recipe for an old-fashioned dock wine.

175g (7 oz) dock root
15g ($^1/_2$ oz) liquorice wood
7g ($^1/_4$ oz) juniper berries
100g (4 oz) raw cane sugar
2 litres ($3^1/_2$ pints) organic red wine

Put all the ingredients together in a china container, cover and place either in a very slow oven or in a bain marie. Continue to heat gently until the mixture is reduced by half. Strain, bottle and seal tightly. Drink a sherry glass of the dock wine every morning for two weeks.

Rosemary in Wine

Steep 6 sprigs of rosemary in a well-sealed bottle of sweet white wine for 14 days. Take 1 wineglass as a daily tonic.

Sage Tonic

Take 100g (4 oz) of fresh sage leaves and put them in a bottle of organic white wine for two weeks. Sweeten to taste with honey and leave for another day. Press and strain through muslin. Bottle, and take 1 sherry glass before lunch and dinner.

You can also infuse sage leaves in boiling water, strain and sweeten with honey for an uplifting sage tea.

Homeopathy

Put most simply, homeopathy is based on the belief that substances that are poisonous in large doses can be beneficial in small doses. Various substances can be taken in the form of pills, capsules, sachets of granules or liquids. These homeopathic remedies can be bought in chemists and health shops, or obtained from a practitioner.

The principles of homeopathy were first expounded in 1796 by a German doctor, Christian Samuel Hahnemann. The fundamental principle that he adopted (and which is still the mainstay of homeopathy) was 'Let like be cured by like'. He discovered that substances that are poisonous or toxic in their natural form can be used to cure, but will cure only that which they cause. Guided by this 'law of healing', Hahnemann first prescribed substantial doses of a remedy, which often severely aggravated the symptoms, even when the eventual outcome was positive. To lessen the initial adverse reactions in his patients, Hahnemann diluted the dosage, using a method of his own devising, and found that this dilution did not diminish the medicinal power of the remedy—but in fact enhanced it.

Many people come to a homeopath for help with a specific symptom: arthritis, asthma, back pain, menstrual problems, migraines, rheumatism, sciatica or skin conditions. The aim of a good homeopath, however, is to do more than simply alleviate the symptom. Homeopathy is directed towards restoring the overall energy balance and treating the condition in a holistic way, so the patient will enjoy increased energy and vitality, better sleep and an improved appetite. With this new feeling of equilibrium will come a natural sense of relaxation.

Homeopathic remedies are derived from a wide variety of sources, which include some pretty unusual substances such as bee stings, snake venoms, arsenic, gold and silica, and even compounds from diseased tissue. Some 2000 different such remedies are in use. Even though these remedies are derived from often dangerous sources, they are completely safe, having been diluted from the original substance (usually in alcohol or water) using Hahnemann's process, known as 'potentation'. Various dilutions are used. A common one is known as 30C, and this indicates a dilution that would be represented by the figure of 1 over 1 followed by 60 noughts (or 1×10^{-60} in scientific notation). It is the use of infinitesimal doses that is the most controversial aspect of homeopathy and the reason why many conventional doctors claim it functions only as a placebo. However, controlled studies have shown the effectiveness of homeopathic medicine in treating a number of diseases.

Taken in this diluted form, homeopathic remedies have no side effects whatsoever and are perfectly safe, non-toxic and non-addictive. They have all been tested extensively on humans (mostly practising homeopaths) to verify their safety and efficacy. Animal testing has never been used in homeopathy.

There is no conflict between conventional medicine and homeopathic remedies and, indeed, both systems of therapy may sometimes be used to complement each other. In most cases, when starting homeopathic treatment you should remain on your current conventional medicine. If you are taking prescribed conventional medicine (whether on prescription or not) you should tell your homeopath, who will discuss the situation with your doctor, if necessary, providing you give permission.

Homeopathy is a holistic therapy—that is, it investigates and treats the whole person rather than the specific problem presented by the patient. Because of this, your homeopath will enquire about many aspects of your condition—not just about the problems you present.

The initial consultation takes about an hour, and the homeopath will wish to hear all your symptoms as well as enquiring about many aspects of your health and way of life. These symptoms will then be analysed and the homeopath will decide upon a specific remedy to suit your particular needs. This analysis could take up to another hour, but you do not have to be present. Once the homeopath has decided on a remedy and potency (dilution) to be recommended, the material will be made up for you personally by the homeopath. The remedy may be provided immediately or it may take a day or two to prepare.

Homeopathy is best when applied to conditions that are reversible—that is, anything that nature can cure or remove. Homeopathy cannot be used in place of surgery, but homeopathic remedies can be taken in conjunction with surgery and can be instrumental in making the surgery safer. They can also hasten post-operative healing.

In their basic form, homeopathic remedies are liquid formulations. They may be prescribed for you in this form, or they can be provided in tablet or granule form. In some cases, creams or lotions may be provided. Normally the form does not affect the action of the remedy, so if you prefer a particular form ask your homeopath. Remedies are taken on the tongue, if liquid, or held in the mouth to dissolve if in solid form. Creams and lotions are for external application. You should not eat or drink for fifteen minutes before or after taking a homeopathic remedy, and you should avoid caffeinated coffee, camphor, menthol, peppermint and similar strong flavours while undergoing homeopathic treatment. Alcohol does not affect homeopathic remedies—unless, of course, they are being taken for problems that are related to it.

Hypnotherapy

Because it can be used to treat conditions in which psychological aspects are important, hypnotherapy is a valuable means of treating stress-related illnesses and so promoting relaxation. It is not clear how hypnosis works, and the links between hypnosis and entertainment have contributed to prejudice against its use as a therapeutic tool.

Increasing numbers of medical and mental health professionals now use hypnosis to overcome the pain of chronic headaches, backaches, childbirth, cancer, severe burns, dental phobias, and more. Some psychologists use hypnosis to overcome bad habits, anxiety, phobias and depression—even to help patients recall past events, although the accuracy of this recall is controversial. Family doctors have begun using hypnosis to treat psychosomatic illness, to control appetite, and to reduce the need for medication, or lower its dosage, in chronic illness.

The history of hypnosis dates back to the 18th century and the work of Frank Anton Mesmer, a physician from Germany. Hypnosis was used as pain relief until anaesthetics became common. Although the word 'hypnosis' comes from the Greek word for sleep, hypnosis is actually an intense state of concentration, and this concentration in focused *inwardly*.

Although different therapists use different hypnosis techniques, the process today often begins with the patient closing his or her eyes and the therapist asking him or her to think relaxing thoughts. Often the patient is asked to imagine a beautiful scene. As the therapist's soothing voice guides the patient down a path of deeper and deeper relaxation, the patient gradually becomes totally focused on the picture he or she sees in the mind—mirroring what happens when the patient is engrossed in a book or a daydream. All outside images and thoughts disappear.

In this state of focused concentration, the patient becomes suggestible. The therapist may then ask the patient to concentrate on his or her own breathing and other sensations inside the body. At this point, the therapist suggests ways in which patients can accomplish individual goals.

The experience of hypnosis in itself should be relaxing, and for someone suffering from an anxiety state or form of depression, it can be used to bring about a soothing sense of relaxation that is a profound relief.

Reflexology

Reflexology is a method for activating the natural healing resources of the body, and many people find it deeply relaxing. Forms of reflexology have been in use for at least 3000 years (paintings depicting the art have been discovered in an Egyptian tomb dating back to 2330 BC). The science of reflexology as it is practised today was developed fairly recently, and its use as a complementary therapy has been on the increase ever since.

Around 1917, an American doctor called William Fitzgerald developed what he called 'zone therapy', which treated the body as being divided into ten zones from head to foot, and asserted that by applying pressure to one area within a zone, one could dull pain in a corresponding area within the same zone.

In the 1930s, Eunice Ingham, an American physiotherapist, concluded in her zone therapy work that some areas of the body were more sensitive than others, the most sensitive of these being the feet. She proceeded to map the entire human body on the tops and bottoms of the feet, eventually discovering that by applying specific pressure with her thumbs and fingers she achieved therapeutic results far beyond simple pain reduction. Eunice Ingham dedicated the remainder of her life to developing and promoting reflexology into the successful complementary treatment it is today.

Reflexology works on the principle that the body is divided into ten zones that run lengthways from head to toe, where the reflex areas for all the organs, glands and body parts are found. The ten body zones are equally split on either side of a vertical, central line. There is a logical arrangement of the pressure points. The thyroid, bladder and stomach are found in the first zone on both feet. Organs on the left side of the body can only be influenced by the left side of the foot. The same rule applies to organs lying to the right of the body. If an organ in a particular zone is unhealthy, there is a chance that the organs within the same zone may be affected too.

Energy, sometimes referred to as qi, kundalini, or the universal life force, also runs through these zones. Reflexologists believe that if this constant flow of energy is impeded by a blockage or congestion, illness sets in. A reflexologist, by using constant, rhythmic pressure on the reflexes of the patient's feet, breaks down the blockage, allowing the return of free-flowing energy and deep relaxation to occur, thus enabling the body's own healing mechanisms to take effect.

Reflexology massage uses small circular movements of the thumb to bring relief. The masseur will massage the zones of the feet and listen to the 'pain' of the client. It is important, however, to differentiate between reflex pain and real pain. You can identify a reflex pain, because it feels as if the foot has been jagged by something sharp or as if the foot is being massaged by a fin-

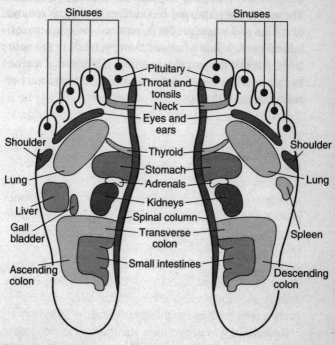

Reflexology zones

gernail. The feeling should make you jump and pull your foot away.

Reflexology has a definite cumulative effect. However, a single session is very relaxing and often invigorating. Since reflexology is so relaxing, there are many benefits to receiving regular reflexology treatment. These include improved blood circulation, the removal of toxins and waste products, reduced tension and revitalized energy. It is a holistic therapy, treating the entire body, not just the part that is ailing. It is a useful method of preventative health care as well as an extremely relaxing form of therapy.

Traditional Chinese Medicine

About 2500 years ago, deep in the mountains of North-ern China, Taoist priests practised Qi Gong—meditative movement revealing and cultivating the vital life force. They believed this force, *qi* (pronounced 'chi' in China, 'ki' in Japan), was inseparable from life itself. They dis-covered that qi animated not only body and earth, but was the energetic force of the entire universe. Tradi-tional Chinese medicine is a philosophy of preserving health, and is based first and foremost on an understand-ing of the ultimate power of qi. In contrast to much of Western medicine, traditional Chinese medicine is a preventative practice, strengthening the immune system to ward off disease.

In traditional Chinese medicine, qi is manifested both as *yin* (cold, dark and 'interior'), and *yang* (warm, light and 'exterior'). In fact, qi is present in all the opposites we experience, such as night and day, hot and cold, growth and decay. And although yin and yang may be perceived as opposites, they are actually inseparable. The recognition of one is essential to the recognition of the other. The balance between them is like the motion of night and day; at the instant darkness reaches its zenith at midnight, the cycle has begun to flow steadily towards dawn. At noon, the zenith of light, the day begins slowly to turn towards the darkness of night. All the internal organs of the body are subject to this nocturnal-diurnal swing of the universe.

This world view further holds that qi, manifesting as yin/yang, makes up the universe in the form of five elements: wood, fire, earth, metal and water. These five elements also represent our bodily constitution as human beings, making us one with the universe. Qi flows into our bodies, up from the earth in its yin form and down from the heavens in its yang form. The energy channels in our bodies through which it moves are called 'meridians'.

These meridians do not directly correspond to any anatomical component recognized by Western medicine. The best way to understand the flow of qi through the meridians is to compare it to the flow of blood in our veins and arteries. If our blood does not reach our toes, they become dead. If our blood does not flow freely, we have high or low blood pressure. If our blood clots, we have an embolism or a stroke. Similarly, unbalanced or stagnant qi can cause many diseases and ailments. In fact, traditional Chinese medicine is based on the principle that every illness, ailment and discomfort in the body can be explained in terms of an imbalance of qi.

Each meridian is related to one of the five elements. For example, the heart meridian is related to the element fire, the kidney and bladder to water. Along the meridians are pressure points, or 'gateways', special places where qi can become blocked. With the help of a trained practitioner, its flow can be freed and balance restored.

Acupuncture

This is a form of traditional Chinese medicine that uses the gentle insertion of hair-fine needles into specific points on the body to stimulate the flow of one's qi, or natural healing energy. As we have already seen, according to ancient Chinese medicine qi flows through the body in channels, known as meridians, and illness is the result of an imbalance of qi.

Most people are surprised to learn that acupuncture needles are very thin (from ten to fifteen acupuncture needles can fit into one conventional needle). Acupuncturists can attain a high level of skill in gently placing these tiny needles into the skin with a minimum of discomfort.

Acupuncture excels in those areas in which conventional medicine offers limited relief—chronic disease, pain control, and stress-related disorders. Acupuncture treatments are drug-free; you avoid side effects or dependency. However you should always inform any practitioner about all pre-existing conditions, the names of all medicines you are taking, whether you are—or could be—pregnant, and if you have a cardiac pacemaker or cosmetic implants. With this information your acupuncturist will be able to ensure the best form of treatment.

Alexander Technique

The Alexander technique is a practical and simple method of learning to focus attention on how we use ourselves during daily activities. F. M. Alexander (1869–1955), an Australian therapist, demonstrated that the difficulties many people experience in learning, in control of performance, and in physical functioning, are caused by unconscious habits. These habits interfere with your natural poise and your capacity to learn. When you stop interfering with the innate coordination of the body, you can take on more complex activities with greater self-confidence and presence of mind. The technique is about learning to bring into our conscious awareness the choices we make, as we make them. Gentle hands-on and verbal instruction reveal the underlying principles of human coordination, allow the student to observe and experience his own habitual patterns, and give the means for release and change.

Most of us are unconsciously armouring ourselves in relation to our environment. This often leaves us feeling anxious, alienated and depressed. Armouring is a deeply unconscious behaviour that has probably gone on since early childhood, maybe even since infancy. Yet it is a habit we can unlearn in the present through careful self-observation. We can unlearn our use of excess tension in our thoughts, movements and relationships.

An Alexander teacher guides a person, as he or she moves, to use less tension. The teacher works by monitoring the student's posture and reminding him or her to implement tiny changes in movement to eradicate the habit of excess tension. Students learn to stop bracing themselves, or to stop collapsing into themselves. As awareness grows, it becomes easier to recognize and relinquish the habit of armouring and dissolve the artificial barriers we put between ourselves and others.

An analogy of this process can be seen in three-dimensional Magic Eye Art. With our ordinary way of looking we see only a mass of dots. When we shift to the 'Magic Eye' way of seeing, a three-dimensional object appears. Through the Alexander technique a similar type of experience is available. But the three-dimensional object we experience is ourself.

Although the Alexander Technique does not treat specific symptoms, you can encourage a marked improvement in overall health, alertness and performance by consciously eliminating harmful habits that cause physical and emotional stress. From an increased, in-depth awareness of how you use your body can come a liberating return to the totally relaxed state of a young child, before unconscious and harmful habits have been learned.

Osteopathy

This is a technique that uses manipulation and massage to help distressed muscles and joints, and make them work more smoothly.

The profession began in 1892 when Andrew Taylor Still, an American farmer, inventor and doctor, opened the USA's first school of osteopathic medicine. He sought alternatives to the medical treatments of his day, which he believed were ineffective as well as often harmful

Still's new philosophy of medicine, based upon the teachings of Hippocrates, advocated that 'Finding health should be the purpose of a doctor. Anyone can find disease.' Like Hippocrates, Still recognized that the human body is a unit in which structure, function, mind and spirit all work together.

Still stressed the importance of preventing disease, eating properly and keeping fit. He studied the body's musculoskeletal system (the muscles, bones and joints) extensively and discovered how it works with other body systems to influence health. He taught that the body has the inherent ability to heal itself when all its systems function in harmony. To support his belief that body structure affects body function—and vice versa—he developed the unique 'hands-on' skill of osteopathic manipulative treatment to diagnose and treat structural problems. He emphasized the compassionate care and treatment of the person as a whole, not as a collection of symptoms or unrelated parts.

The philosophy and practices of A. T. Still, considered radical in the 1800s, are generally accepted principles of good medicine today.

Psychotherapy

Therapy involving discussion between patient and client need not be organized by a doctor specializing in mental illness, and the client undergoing the therapy need not be mentally ill. He or she may just feel that there is something wrong with life and be seeking help, or someone who knows the person may well have recommended such a course of action. The person in charge of the therapy programme will not be a psychiatrist but a psychoanalyst or psychotherapist.

A word of warning is necessary here for anyone contemplating this kind of therapy. Psychiatrists are qualified doctors, usually attached to a hospital, and people are usually referred to them by a general practitioner. You can have confidence, therefore, in his or her training, even if you do not get on with the actual person. This is not the case, however, with all psychotherapists.

Many psychotherapists hold a suitable professional qualification, such as a degree in psychology, and some may even be medical doctors, but there is nothing to prevent anyone setting up in business without such qualifications. Some people would argue that it is the skills of the therapist, not the qualifications, that count, but it is as well to check up on the nature of these skills first.

Many general practitioners will be able to make a recommendation. Failing this, do try to get hold of a personal recommendation from someone who has previously attended, and been satisfied with the psychotherapist. An attempt has been made to set up a register for therapists, and you could probably obtain details of this from your local library. You must feel that you can trust the person to whom you are entrusting your mind.

To some extent the skills required by the psychotherapist are those required by the successful psychiatrist. For a start, they must have good listening skills and have the ability to get people to talk about themselves, without revealing any reaction of condemnation or shock. Both need skill in interpreting what they hear from the client.

Often the problems that the clients of a psychotherapist have are not too dissimilar from those of the patients of a psychiatrist. Sometimes the difference is only one of degree. For example, two different people might feel that something is not right in their lives and might put this fact down to a bad relationship with a parent—sometimes physical or sexual abuse might be involved—but it is the extent to which this has affected the individual and what he or she decides to do about it that makes the difference.

One may become completely obsessed with the problem—something like the death of a parent, or the birth of a child may set this off. His or her mind ceases to be able to function in the way it normally does, and he or she becomes mentally ill. Medical help has to be sought, and the general practitioner recommends referral to a psychiatrist.

Another person who has much the same problem may not be mentally affected by it to nearly the same extent but may be conscious of the effect it is having on his or her life—perhaps he or she is having difficulties in forming lasting relationships. The person realizes that help must be sought and thinks of psychotherapy.

The basis of modern psychoanalysis and psychotherapy goes back to the Austrian psychiatrist Sigmund Freud, the inventor of psychoanalysis. The disciplines seek to tap into the subconscious of the individual undergoing analysis or therapy and to release any hidden fears and to unblock any repressed emotions. By this means, people seek to discover more about themselves.

The major difference between psychoanalysis and psychotherapy is that, as the name suggests, the latter seeks to heal. The suppressed fears and emotions that emerge from analysis are not an end in themselves but a means by which the healing process may be begun. By unblocking the subconscious, the therapist tries to help the client towards a better understanding of himself or herself and to help him or her cope more effectively with life in the light of this understanding.

The role of the psychotherapist is to listen and interpret what the client is saying. Some people feel that simply talking to a complete stranger is, in fact, therapeutic. Friends and members of the family may be too involved, over-emotional, or even condemnatory or judgmental, and are often too busy to really listen. The psychotherapist is someone who is totally uninvolved and detached, whose good opinion or otherwise does not matter, and who has time to listen. Furthermore— and this is an important part of psychotherapy—the talking can go on over a longish period of time, often quite a few months, so that there is no sense of rush. There is plenty of time to explore past experiences and relationships. The person with a problem feels that at last there is someone there to listen and help.

The basic aim of analysis and therapy may not vary from one therapist to another, but the method of approach does. Some of them are closer to the techniques of Freud than others and advocate that clients say anything that comes into their heads, using a kind of free association as a means of unblocking the unconscious. Other therapists may prompt the client with a few gentle leading questions, especially as a means of getting each session started.

Some adopt a more formal, traditional approach than

others and ask the client to lie on a sofa in such a way that he or she is unable to see the therapist. External stimuli are reduced to a minimum in an effort to get the client to concentrate as much as possible on his or her own thoughts. Others regard this as being too rigid an approach and choose to talk to their clients in a less formal setting, although the therapists themselves are never intrusive.

Many people find psychotherapy a very useful and rewarding therapy. At the very least they can talk about things they have never dreamt of speaking about before and can learn to face up to them. They can learn to come to terms with the past and be able to reach some understanding of how the past, with its suppressed fears and emotions, has effected their present and prevented them living life to the full. People can feel much more comfortable with themselves, and be able to go forward in a much more relaxed and confident way to build a future.

Useful Addresses

Stress Centres
First Assist
Britannia House
50 Great Charles Street
Queensway
Birmingham B3 2LP

Centre for Stress Management
156 Westcombe Hill
London SE3 7DH

Counselling Services
British Association of Counselling
1 Regent Place
Rugby
Warwickshire CV21 2PJ

MIND (National Association for
Mental Health)
15-19 Broadway
Stratford E15 UBQ

Samaritans
10 The Grove
Slough
Berks SL1 1QP
(or look up your local phone book)

Complementary Medicine
Institute for Complementary
Medicine
PO Box 194
London SE16 1QZ
(publishes a full register of
complementary therapists)

Natural Health Network
Chardstock House
Chard Somerset
TA20 2TL

Council for Complementary and
Alternative Medicine
Park House
206-208 Latimer Road
London W10 6RE

British Holistic Medical Association
179 Gloucester Place
London NW1 6DX

Acupuncture
Association of Chinese Acupuncture/Traditional Chinese
Medicine International (Registered UK/China)
International School of Natural
Medicine/BIFRAN (British and
International Federation Register
and Association of Naturopathy)
Prospect House
2 Grove Lane
Retford
Nottingham
DN22 6NA
(provides patients' clinics,
education and registration in
Chinese acupuncture, moxibustion
and massage)

College of Traditional Acupuncture
Tao House
Queensway
Royal Leamington Spa
Warwickshire

British Acupuncture Council
Park House
206 Latimer Road
London W10 6RE

Alexander Technique
Professional Association of
  Alexander Teachers
14 Kingsland
Jesmond
Newcastle-upon-Tyne
NE2 3AL

Aromatherapy
International Federation of
  Aromatherapists
Stanford House
2-4 Chiswick High Road
London
W4 1TH

Autogenic Training Therapy
British Association for Autogenic
  Training and Therapy
86 Harley Street
London
W1N 1AE

Holistic Massage
Massage Training Institute
24 Highbury Grove
London
N5 2EA

Homeopathy
The Homeopathic Trust
15 Clerkenwell Close
London EC1R 0AA

Society of Homeopaths
2 Artizan Road
Northampton NN1 4HU
(register of qualified professional
homoeopaths)

United Kingdom Homeopathic
  Medical Association
Administration Office
6 Livingstone Road Gravesend
Kent DA12 5DZ

Hypnotherapy
British Society of Clinical
  Hypnotherapists
229a Sussex Gardens
Lancaster Gate
London W2 2RL
(for a nationwide list of practition-
ers)

Nutritional Therapy
Society for the Promotion of
  Nutritional Therapy (SPNT)
PO Box 47
Heathfield
East Sussex TN21 8ZX
(send SAE and £1.00 for
information and a list of nutri-
tional therapists)

Institute for Optimum Nutrition
Blades Court
Deodar Road
London SW15 2NU

Achieving Relaxation

Osteopathy
Natural Theraputic Osteopathic
 Society
14 Marford Road
 Wheathampstead
Herts AL4 8AS

Psychovisual Therapy
Psychovisual Therapy Association
P.O. Box 1193
Poole
Dorset

Reflexology
Association of Reflexologists
27 Old Gloucester Street
London WC1 3XX

British Reflexology Association
Monks Orchard
Whitborne
Worcester WR6 5RB
(register of members £2; for
details of courses, books, charts
send SAE)

Shiatsu
The European Shiatsu Network
Highbanks, Lockeridge,
 Marlborough
Wiltshire SN8 4TQ

Yoga
British Wheel of Yoga
1 Hamilton Place
Boston Road
Sleaford
Lincolnshire NG34 7ES